WEALTH

HOW THE RICH GET RICH
AND HOW YOU CAN TOO

THOMAS M. GILBRIDE

ISBN-10: 1453824278
EAN-13: 9781453824276
Library of Congress Control Number: 2010914465

DEDICATION

This book is dedicated to my eight sons.
They have enriched my life immeasurably.

TABLE OF CONTENTS

Prologue

Throughout history, money and wealth have been con-troversial. For some, money and wealth are good; for others, they're evil. The famous biblical admonition (I Timothy 6-10), "For the love of money is the root of all evil," warns us about the dangers of wealth. To love money for its own sake creates all manner of evil, according to St. Paul. Virtue is found in lov-ing God and one another. It's found in the good we do, not the wealth we acquire.

The lack of money is the root of all evil, according to George Bernard Shaw. Shaw's comments point out the misery poverty produces and the desperation of want.

"Capital as such is not evil; it is its wrong use that is evil. Capital in some form or other will always be needed." On the other hand, Gandhi believed money is neither good nor evil; it's an elementary and useful necessity.

Here is yet another perspective on money. "A feast is made for laughter, and wine maketh merry: but money answereth all things. "Ecclesiastes 10:19

Pursuing wealth and money has its proponents and detractors. Wealth can be an agent for good or evil. Money can corrupt people or can ennoble them. On its own, money is a utility, a useful device we need to engage in society and the economic realities of daily living. People need money to live, and the more you have the better you can live.

To possess a great deal of money is empowering. Often, it's needed to seize opportunity. It makes you self reliant and gives you more options and choices in life. It's a resource that can be used for productive purposes and progress.

This book addresses the necessity of having an adequate supply of money and wealth in your personal life and the practical role it plays. Acquiring money and wealth is important and it's entirely possible for more people to acquire more of it. It's entirely possible for more people to become millionaires. Wealth and its acquisition aren't reserved for an elite few—they are available to all. Those of us who are interested in making personal prosperity a part of our lives should pursue money and wealth for the right reasons and use them wisely.

PREFACE

The late billionaire J. Paul Getty gave sage advice when he answered a question about how you can acquire wealth. His advice was to rise early, work hard, and strike oil. I'll discuss this quote again later. As you'll see, the part about discovering oil is critical. Much advice and many books about success, including ones written about financial success, come from successful people like Getty. They pass along their stories, insights, observations, and advice so readers can use the information as a means of becoming successful. After all, who better to talk about success than those who are successful themselves? These people are speaking from personal experience, and their accomplishments lend credibility to their words. A good example is the *Autobiography of Benjamin Franklin*, which is considered by many to be the best self-help book ever written. Franklin wrote it late in life, after he was an astounding success.

Other success books are written by observers or researchers about people other than themselves. Notable examples are *How to Win Friends and Influence People* by Dale Carnegie, *Think and Grow Rich* by Napoleon Hill, *The 7 Habits of Highly Effective People* by Stephen Covey, *Rich Dad, Poor Dad* by Robert T. Kiyosaki, and *The Millionaire Next Door* by Thomas T. Stanley and William D. Danko. The list of notable examples goes on. These books are based on research and observations. Likewise, this book isn't about me. It's about the wealthy people I came to know through my work as a financial adviser and is based on my work with a large number of high-income, high-net-worth clients over a thirty-year period. These observations about wealthy people and how they acquired wealth are augmented by research I conducted to develop several lectures for various professional continuing education courses.

During my financial planning career, I was associated closely with many millionaires. I knew these people well and had an intimate understanding of their overall financial affairs. I knew their stories. I saw, firsthand, how they acquired their wealth, and in some cases, how they lost it. It was a unique education for me. It was clear from this experience there are many roads to personal wealth and prosperity. These people came from all walks of life and many different socioeconomic groups. They had different levels of education and varying degrees of intelligence. Their individual talents and skills were equally diverse, but they all engaged in activities that led to the acquisition of personal wealth. These activities, which are what this book is about, can create prosperity in your life, too.

This book follows a simple formula. First, I identify the wealthy among us, those who have acquired a million dollars or more of personal wealth, and group them into specific categories according to the wealth creating activities that made them rich. Second, I describe those wealth-creating activities. I focus on the twelve situations and activities that provide and produce above-average personal wealth—substantial wealth. I describe each as a road or route. I try to make it clear each is a road many successful people have traveled before. I go on to provide information about traveling and navigating each of these roads to help you decide which road you can travel successfully. Finally, I emphasize those roads that are accessible to most people. I show you the way and provide insight into what it takes to succeed in each of these endeavors.

In addition to providing a comprehensive overview about how millionaires acquire their wealth, I discuss personal character, behavior, and other factors, which many commentators have identified as factors responsible for acquiring wealth and success in life.

But the primary message in this book is that it's what the rich choose to do that makes them rich. The roads they travel are important. Where one successfully endeavors in the right enterprise, wealth follows. Notable personal character and exemplary behavior in a fruitless enterprise may garner praise and admiration, but economic prosperity doesn't follow. To acquire wealth, you must endeavor in an enterprise that has the potential to produce wealth.

Many of us, including those who've become millionaires, have failed at one thing or another in life. Success often comes after one fails, perhaps several times. A book about financial success that doesn't address failure ignores reality. If a book illuminates the upside potential of a particular activity but neglects to elaborate about the risks and odds, it's incomplete.

Therefore, I discuss the good, the bad, and the ugly aspects of engaging in a particular activity.

No one travels all twelve roads presented in this book, but some end up traveling several, perhaps one after another, or several simultaneously. Although each road can lead to financial success, you may not succeed in a particular endeavor. If so, try again, perhaps by taking another route. It's important to succeed financially because financial success will largely define the quality of your life.

If you're reading this book, it's likely you want wealth and prosperity to be part of your life. If so, the Millionaire's Club is your destination. Knowing your destination gives you a big advantage. Now you simply need to get on a road that will take you there. This book is your guide.

ACKNOWLEDGMENT

I owe a great debt of gratitude to my son, Brian. Without his enthusiasm and encouragement, this book would have never been written.

I humbly acknowledge Almighty God, from whom all things, including the wealth of nations and personal prosperity, proceed.

INTRODUCTION

"Some Kind of Wonderful"
—song title, Grand Funk Railroad

What's it like to have all the money you need for the things you need when you need them? What's it like never to worry about money? What's it like to write a check to a friend, or even a stranger, simply because he or she needs the money and you want to help? What's it like to have so much money that money doesn't matter anymore? What's it like when you have so much money you can purchase almost anything, do almost anything, or go almost anywhere whenever you want? In such a state, you'd be free like few other people are free. What's that like? You choose the superlative you like best. For me, an old

Grand Funk Railroad song title comes to mind—"It's Some Kind of Wonderful."

The foregoing describes the rich among us—the wealthy. Such people are millionaires and enjoy the privileges that come along with millionaire status. "Membership has its privileges." In American advertising, that phrase was once a slogan for the American Express card. Some of you may remember it; but for those who don't, the message was that an American Express cardholder could purchase almost anything money could buy, including the finer things in life. But not everyone could qualify for an American Express card. Qualifying for the card was itself a privilege, and it opened the door to countless other privileges. It was a key to the good life.

One thing a credit card won't buy you, however, is membership in the Millionaire's Club. You need a million dollars of net worth for that. Membership in the Millionaire's Club provides a measure of financial security and independence few Americans enjoy. Losing a job isn't devastating to a millionaire. When the CEO of a major public company loses his or her job, he or she may be worried about his or her reputation, but he or she won't be worried about paying the electric bill next month. The wealth that comes with holding executive-level positions ensures your financial security and independence. People with money can purchase items they need without having to sacrifice regular trips to the grocery store. Millionaire status enhances your independence too. It could free you from the necessity of working altogether. Financial security and independence, and the happiness and quality of life they create, are, perhaps, the most significant benefits of being a millionaire.

Membership enables you to take advantage of opportunities when they present themselves. When opportunity knocks, you can take advantage of it because you have money. If an emergency strikes, you can deal with it without sacrificing other assets, such as your home or retirement funds.

Being a millionaire creates a certain amount of justifiable pride and personal satisfaction. It also allows you to do things most people can not even consider—such as retiring early, traveling the world, buying what you want when you want, or engaging in charity and philanthropy—that might not be possible otherwise.

Bill Gates is one of the wealthiest men in the world. He's the poster boy for big philanthropy. The amount of money Gates and his wife Melinda have given to improve the overall well-being of humanity is astounding. How cool is that? Being a philanthropist can be gratifying and fun. Make no mistake: Americans are very charitable, even those who aren't wealthy. But wealthy people have an opportunity few of us have—they have more money than they need, and many of them give boatloads of it away to help others.

Generally, life is better with an adequate supply of money. Your quality of life will be determined, in part, by the amount of money you have. Do you have all the money you need? Could you use a little more money? There aren't many of us who have too much money.

The United States is the most successful nation in the history of the world. Why do we live and work in a country that has produced more billionaires and millionaires than any country in history, yet most of us would say we could use more money? Why aren't more of us millionaires? Is it inevitable in a capitalistic economy only a fortunate few acquire wealth? Or do those who acquire millions of dollars in personal wealth take steps the rest of us don't? One thing is clear. Those who acquire

wealth spend their time and effort in endeavors that have legitimate wealth-creating potential.

The architects of our nation combined democracy with
capitalism. That recipe produces wealth and prosperity for individuals and the nation as a whole. People can flourish and
thrive in such an environment. However, only 2 percent of the
population has financial assets of a million dollars or more, and
less than 10 percent has a net worth of a million dollars or more.
So, on one hand, while all of us enjoy the nation's prosperity in
many ways, including access to schools, social security, health
care and highways, few of us own much in the way of personal
wealth. Few of us are millionaires.

Forty percent of the personal wealth in America is owned by
one percent of the population, and 95 percent of all personal wealth
is owned by 50 percent of us. That leaves 5 percent of property and
assets for the other 50 percent of the population. When you hear
people talking about the haves and have-nots, these are the two
groups, roughly 50-50, to whom they're referring.

Before the economic recession that started in 2007, the
median net worth per household in the United States was
about $120,000, including home equity. Who knows what it
is now. With home values down by one-third in some places
and 401(k) values still making a comeback from a 40 percent
or more decline, even this modest amount of wealth has been
whittled down, in many cases, by more than half. Nonetheless,
when we examine the big picture, we see an affluent society.
But when we scrutinize the picture, we see it consists of individuals with varying degrees of wealth, including those with
little or no wealth.

Why is it after spending much of our lives working to make
a living and get ahead, there are so few millionaires? Why is

that the case amid such prosperity? Can the typical American, the average person, become a millionaire? Some say no, arguing if the typical person had more money, he or she would simply consume it foolishly or in some form of self-indulgence rather than creating wealth or long-term financial security. Others say yes, arguing one can live comfortably and well and still accumulate wealth if he or she makes smart choices.

Democracy and capitalism are the platform on which we live. The platform is well equipped, providing individuals the opportunity to prosper. Yet in the pursuit of prosperity, we have a few big winners, a large number of runners-up, and millions of people who are at the bottom in terms of accumulating personal wealth. The information in this book will enable more individuals to take advantage of the opportunities available to all.

"You are here." We're all familiar with the signs we find in public places indicating our locations. Right now, you're somewhere in your economic life, and knowing where you are allows you to navigate where you wish to go. Are you a millionaire? It's unlikely a millionaire would read this book, but if you are a millionaire, you probably achieved millionaire status by traveling one of the twelve roads I describe in the following pages. If not, you'll want to learn more about the twelve routes that lead to riches. If you're not a millionaire, it's important to become one, as you'll see. Knowing the way gives you a huge advantage and dramatically improves your chances for success. The journey begins now.

CHAPTER 1

THE IMPORTANCE OF BEING A MILLIONAIRE

Money is better than poverty, if only for financial reasons.
                                        – Woody Allen

Woody Allen had it right. We all need money for financial reasons. In any modern society, you can't live without money, and the more money you have, the better you live. Your well-being will be compromised quickly if you're short of money. Money is elementary. It's fundamental to sustaining yourself and is required to accomplish any number of things. Without money, some things simply can't be accomplished.

But needing money for financial reasons is only part of the story. We need money for happiness too. Thomas Jefferson acknowledged a person needed to be free and enjoy modest prosperity to be happy. Freedom and poverty aren't a formula for happiness. Prosperity, a little wealth, goes a long way to contributing to personal happiness. Furthermore, almost everyone wants a better life for himself or herself and his or her family. A better life is the American dream. There are many elements that contribute to creating a better life, and money is one of them.

Our right to life, liberty, and the pursuit of happiness is guaranteed by the U.S. Constitution. Our founding fathers recognized humankind has certain unalienable and self-evident rights. Recognizing these rights and creating a system that enables people to pursue their self-interests and happiness is an amazing achievement in human affairs. Were it not for the insidious provisions that allowed slavery to exist where human freedom was to flourish, the founding documents of the United States would've been an unquestionable masterpiece. Fortunately, those flaws have been remedied.

Making money and accumulating wealth may not be of interest to some people, but the absence of adequate wealth can create misery. Everyone wants happiness and a fulfilling life. Hoping for happiness and working for a better life has been a part of the human condition for centuries. Throughout most of human history, the average person devoted himself or herself to a daily quest for sustenance and survival. In the modern age, democracy and capitalism have created a beacon of hope and a better life for countless millions throughout the world.

In America, people are free to pursue their own interests without the threat of interference from a conqueror, monarchy, religion, dictator, or government. People can own property, get an education and enjoy a higher standard of living. They can acquire wealth. Even in an age of globalization, in which economic opportunities exist in many parts of the world, America continues to be the great hope for a better life.

A better life means different things to different people. For some, it's religious freedom. For others, it's the right to privacy. Yet others seek a better standard of living. Public schools, roads and parks, and world-class health care and social programs, such as Social Security and Medicare, constitute the quality of life many desire. For some, it's economic opportunity and the right to engage in business activities. A better life is all of these societal elements and more.

The more we attain and acquire, the more we want, such as a bigger home in a better neighborhood and better schools for our children. Wanting more and better is part of the human condition.

Those who have a poor quality of life want to improve it. Likewise, those who have a good life want the same thing. The American dream is an evolving phenomenon and continues to grow. Throughout time, the elements that constitute a better life are represented by an increasing list of our desires. The American dream covers a lot of territory.

Two elements of the American dream too few of us have acquired are financial security and financial independence. A comprehensive list of the elements that constitute a better life would include financial security at a minimum and ideally financial independence. Financial security means having enough money to purchase what you need when you need it. It means not worrying about money. Financial independence means having not only enough money to purchase what you need, but what you want too. Both require a million dollars or more of personal net worth. If you had more money, you'd have more financial security and independence. You'd have a better life.

Let's put things into perspective. Money shouldn't be the most important thing in life. For one, it can corrupt. The old biblical adage, "The love of money is the root of all evil," is true. The pursuit of money can bring tragedy into a person's life too. Money is simply a medium of exchange, a storehouse for wealth, a means of satisfying a debt or obligation. It's a means of acquiring a benefit. An adequate supply of money improves lives, and that's why it's so important. Chances are a poor person will live better and be happier if he or she has more money. If you remove money from the life of a wealthy person, he or she won't live as well and is likely to be unhappy or at least not as happy.

The right to be free and pursue happiness is a birthright. Where you pursue happiness, you must pursue prosperity too. Happiness without some wealth is still poverty. Worry and want, because of a lack of money, infringe on your peace of mind and may destroy your happiness.

The good news about acquiring wealth is we live in an economic environment that creates wealth. The U.S. economy has produced millions of millionaires and more billionaires than any other in the world. This wealth-creating machine is indifferent to people and doesn't care who you are or where you're from. It rewards those who successfully endeavor in wealth-creating activities. If you want to create lifetime financial security for yourself and your family, you need to become a millionaire. If you want to enjoy financial independence, you need to become a multimillionaire. There has never been another place on earth where so many people have had the opportunity to do so, and that's likely to continue for the foreseeable future.

BY THE NUMBERS

Here are a few representative or composite numbers that support the proposition you should be striving for membership in the Millionaire's Club. Take a closer look at the definition of financial security, which has two elements. The first is adequate passive income, the kind you receive without having to work for it. Essentially, financial security is achieved when a person (or household) has enough income from passive sources to allow that person to pay for his or her standard of living and the things he or she needs. It might take $50,000 a year for one person to buy what he or she needs and cover his or her living expenses. It might take $25,000 for another person. It might take $100,000 for yet another. But whatever the number, a financially secure person has enough income from retirement plans, social security, interest, investment income, trusts, or distributions from business sources to pay for his or her needs and living expenses. The second element is peace of mind. A financially secure person doesn't worry about money because he or she has what he or she needs. Most of us want financial security.

Financial independence takes financial security to a higher level. A person (or household) is financially independent when he or she can pay for his or her standard of living and what he or she needs with passive income and still has money available to purchase what he or she wants. Money isn't an issue for such a person because he or she has plenty of it. A financially independent person can pretty much do what he or she wants and go where he or she wants when he or she wants.

There are two elements that constitute financial independence. First, a financially independent person has an excess supply of money, more than he or she needs to pay for his or her standard of living and to purchase what he or she needs. This excess money can be used for whatever discretionary purposes he or she chooses. Like the financially secure person, the financially independent person doesn't worry about money. He or she actually enjoys the money he or she has, what he or she can do with it and what it can do for him or her and others.

Financial security and independence set a person free. An adequate passive income frees a person from the necessity of working to make a living. That's important because most people earn the money they need to live by working, but when a person can no longer work because of a job loss, there's no work available, he or she is too sick or too old, or he or she wishes to stop working and retire he or she needs to rely upon a passive income to replace his or her wages. The sooner someone acquires enough income-producing assets to support his or her standard of living, without working, the better. You can continue to work by choice, but once you reach this level, work becomes optional and you can do what you want.

Take Benjamin Franklin, for example. He worked for a living and owned a printing business. He sold his printing business at age forty-two and had enough income to sustain himself and his family, so he was free to do whatever he wanted. What did he do? He became the most esteemed scientist of his day. Because he was financially independent, he was able to serve his country, contribute to drafting of the Constitution, and become a central figure in the American Revolution. His achievements, even by today's standards, are astounding. He was able to accomplish so much, in part, because he enjoyed economic freedom. He had a passive income and assets and wasn't shackled by the daily need to make a living. Money set him free. It has set thousands of others free and can set you free.

So how much money does it take to create financial security? The average wage earner in the United States makes about $30,000 a year. If you have two average wage earners in a household, you have $60,000 of annual household income. Census data indicates the four-member household has the highest median income in the country at about $64,000 a year. The median income, according to the Federal Reserve Bank, for all households in 2007 was $50,233. The numbers for those who are retired is less. They range from $15,000 to $36,000 a year, depending on the source and nature of the data.

A 2008 study about middle-class adults released by the Pew Research Center in Washington stated median household income was $50,811. This matches up closely with the 2007 Federal Reserve Bank number noted above. The study cited 53 percent of adults consider themselves middle income, 25 percent consider themselves lower income, and 21 percent consider themselves upper income. These numbers may not be representative of you, or people you know, but they're useful because they are representative of a household with an annual income in the middle of all incomes.

I have read and reviewed various surveys and studies about financial security throughout the years. The data suggests about half of us enjoy financial security. This includes all adult age groups. The other half of us are short of money. About half of us represent the haves in society. This group is doing well financially. Some in this group are doing absolutely great. There are few money worries among the haves, and life, in general, is good. The other half of us are the have-nots. This group has periodic to daily concerns about money. Many in this group struggle with financial issues.

In a recent survey of retired people, those who had the largest annual income, more than $75,000 a year, reported they were very satisfied with retirement. There was a much smaller incidence of satisfied retirees among those who had less than $50,000 of annual retirement income. The survey concluded, among other things, money buys happiness, at least in retirement.

Let's round the Pew study number and assume annual income for a *typical* person or household is $50,000 a year. I'll use this number as a benchmark and assume it is the threshold income needed for the average, or typical, person to create financial security in his or her life. This typical household is on the dividing line between the haves and the have-nots. An income above this level creates more financial security and approaches financial independence. Below this level there is less or little financial security and more worry.

We'll assume a typical person will use all this money to support his or her standard of living. This is income before payroll and income taxes, so we're looking at about roughly $44,000 of after-tax disposable income. That represents $3,337 a month to pay for his or her standard of living and other expenses.

Different households spend the same level of income differently. There are plenty of folks who'd spend this sum each month on what they'd consider to be mainstream expenses, nothing extravagant. A quick look at bank statements of people with this level of monthly income would verify it's easy to spend this sum of money every month on what would be considered normal living expenses. Some households with this income would save a portion of it, and some would spend more and consequently incur debt.

People maintaining households in a geographic area where the cost of living is less than the median income cited in the Pew study may not worry about money. In situations like this, those households may be able to comfortably pay for their standard of living and expenses and enjoy peace of mind. There may even be a little money left over. Those people living in households where the cost of living is higher than the $50,811 cited in the Pew study would find that living standards would have to be reduced or debts would begin to accumulate. There is less peace of mind in such circumstances. Those people would have to earn more or spend less to make ends meet. Earning enough to cover living expenses and to pay for a household's standard of living is why there are so many two income households today. For many, one income is simply not enough. People often move so they can earn more money. Others move to lower their cost of living. A person earning $50,000 per year and living in New York City is going to find that it is difficult to make ends meet each month. If that same person were to move to Portsmouth, Ohio he or she would find that a $50,000 per year income goes a lot further.

Since the personal savings rate in America is low, given the cost of living and the typical American lifestyle, we'll assume nothing is saved. All of this income would be spent each month paying bills and on living expenses.

Millions of us get up every morning and go to work to acquire enough money to maintain, and hopefully improve, our standard of living. We work for financial reasons—to pay the bills—hoping we'll arrive at a point in life where we can stop working, with sufficient income to support a comfortable standard of living. Most people plan on retiring sometime in their sixties. When they retire, they don't want to worry about money. They want peace of mind and financial security. Once a typical person is no longer working, maintaining his or her standard of living is almost impossible without a passive income that will pay for his or her standard of living and expenses and the assets that will produce it.

Using our $50,000 benchmark for average household income—representative of a typical household's expenditure for living expenses—as well as accepting this income as the threshold for financial security and peace of mind, it would take one million dollars or more of assets to produce the $50,000 annual income needed. This assumes a person can get a 5 percent annual return on his or her assets.

Considering how low interest rates are, it may be difficult to buy into the idea of earning a consistent return of 5 percent on your assets. Interest rates fluctuate throughout time. From a historical perspective, average returns on high-quality corporate bonds have been 5 percent or greater. Likewise, the dividends on many high-quality stocks are well above 5 percent. Earning a 5 percent return is a reasonable expectation. If you can't get a 5 percent return on your assets then you'll need more than a million dollars to generate a $50,000 annual income.

Retirement plans and social security count. These resources will reduce the amount of income-producing assets you need for financial security. When you have a $50,000 passive income from social security and employer pensions, you don't need to have a net worth of one million dollars. You have the income a million dollars will generate—the equivalent of a million dollars of assets earning a 5 percent return. Under these circumstances you become *the equivalent millionaire*.

Financial planners and retirement advisers tell their clients not to consume their assets during their lifetime because they'll end up poor. Instead, they should plan on having enough assets to allow them to pay for their living expenses and other spending without drawing down more than 3 to 5 percent of their assets each year (this sum includes interest, investment income, and principal if necessary). At 3 percent, you'd need to have assets of $1,666,667 to provide an annual income of $50,000. It is unlikely that you would run out of money at this rate. At 4 percent, it would take $1,250,000 of assets. If you want to maintain a standard of living throughout your lifetime that costs more than $50,000 a year, you'll need more than a million dollars. Because of inflation, younger people need to think in terms of acquiring $4 million to $5 million. Even a retired person will have to cope with inflation during retirement. Everyday expenses can double easily during retirement, and the cost of health care may continue to rise at a rate higher than inflation.

Some people live on much less than $50,000 a year, and that's all they need or want. In this case, a person doesn't need to be a millionaire. As long as he or she can remain healthy and avoid any serious financial issues, he or she will be fine. Otherwise, he or she may be miserable.

Some argue that as people grow older, they need less income to maintain their living standard. That may be true for some, but there are thousands of people who approach retirement realizing they need to maintain their income to preserve their quality of life. People also are concerned about outliving their money or losing everything to medical and long-term care expenses. There's little peace of mind for those in such circumstances. No one wants to run out of money.

Today, a person age sixty-five should plan on having enough money to last twenty to thirty years because that's how long, on average, people are living today. People who are younger than age sixty-five will live even longer. In our example, the median $50,000 annual income needed to support an average standard of living requires one million dollars of assets earning a 5 percent return. According to numbers published by the Federal Reserve Bank for 2007, the median household net worth in the United States was $120,300. That's well short of a million dollars.

According to a study conducted for the AARP, the average net worth for those age sixty-five and older is $558,000. In the severe economic climate we're in at the moment that number has declined. But in any case, a 5 percent return on $558,000 produces an annual income of only $27,500, assuming all of the $558,000 is available to produce income.

Social Security alone will not replace a $50,000 income. The average monthly Social Security benefit check in 2009 was $1,153 ($13,836 annually). Employer pensions are vanishing. In 1974 more than three hundred thousand employers offered their employees a pension (lifetime income). Currently, fewer than twenty-five thousand employers do so. More of us are on our own when it comes to creating financial security. Most of us are nowhere close to having the assets we need to replace our wages when we stop working. More of us need to be millionaires. Remember, less than 10 percent of us have a million dollars or more of assets.

If it takes a million dollars of income-producing assets to achieve financial security, how much does it take to become financially independent? If it takes a million dollars of investment assets to generate the income required to support a typical standard of living, then another $500,000 of assets would provide $25,000 (before taxes) more for discretionary spending. Another million would double a typical person's income, providing as much mad money as needs money. In the end, it comes down to standard of living and lifestyle. A typical person needs at least another $500,000 to $1,000,000 of income-producing assets to be financially independent. He or she needs to be a multimillionaire. Think how much independence $5 million to $10 million would buy. How about $1 billion or $2 billion?

We all need money for financial reasons and we'll need it throughout our entire lifetime, particularly when we stop working. But of equal importance is happiness. If you want to be happy, or at least improve your chances for happiness, and if you want a better life, financial security that lasts a lifetime, the enjoyment and satisfaction financial independence brings, and the economic freedom money can provide, you need to be a millionaire or possess the equivalent income that a million-dollar net worth provides.

Think about a $50,000 annual income in terms of your own situation. Is it enough to provide you with the standard of living and peace of mind you desire? Remember, it takes a million dollars or more of income-producing assets to create the income needed to support an average standard of living.

Think about having all the money you need and then some. How much would it take to set you free? What's your number?

But is it possible? Can anyone become a millionaire? Well, this is America, and America has produced more millionaires and billionaires than any other place ever. And in America, there's equal opportunity for all.

CHAPTER 2

THE MILLIONAIRES AND TWELVE ROADS TO RICHES

If I had a $1,000,000, I'd be rich.
– Song title and lyric, Barenaked Ladies

Millionaires are a cross section of society and come from all walks of life. If we start at the top of the list, there's an elite group of high-profile billionaires. Forbes Magazine publishes a list of billionaires annually. In a typical year Warren Buffett, chief executive officer and chairman of Berkshire Hathaway, and Bill Gates, one of the founders of Microsoft, compete for the No. 1 spot. This year Carlos Slim of Mexico tops the list. But Gates and Buffett are perennially at the top of the list of the wealthiest people in the United States and typically the world. Their individual wealth fluctuates between $50 billion and $62 billion each. The family of the late Sam and Helen Walton is, collectively, among the wealthiest families on earth—worth about $100 billion. Some folks with famous last names, such as Rockefeller, DuPont, Kennedy, and Hilton, enjoy millionaire status too. There's old wealth that has remained in families for decades, and centuries, for that matter. Many royal families and monarchies throughout the world possess vast amounts of personal wealth.

In the popular book, *The Millionaire Next Door*, Thomas Stanley and William Danko point out many millionaires are anonymous. They live in regular neighborhoods, have ordinary jobs, go to regular places and do ordinary things. They don't eat caviar, drink champagne regularly, drive expensive cars, or belong to private clubs. They're ordinary people who have a million-dollar net worth. When we pass them on the street, we don't suspect they're millionaires and many of them like it that way. They may have a mainstream standard of living too, but, unlike regular folks, they have financial security and independence.

Harland David "Colonel" Sanders, the founder of Kentucky Fried Chicken, was a regular guy. So was Wendy's founder Dave Thomas, who started out as an army cook. Sanders, Thomas, McDonald's Ray Kroc, Apple Computer's Steve Jobs, and J. K. Rowling, the author of Harry Potter books, all were regular folks who became multimillionaires. Colonel Sanders not only created the Kentucky Fried Chicken brand, he contributed to launching the fast-food industry. Sam Walton was an enterprising young man with the benefit of a Wharton (School of Business, University of Pennsylvania) education who turned his 5-and-10-cent store into the world's largest retailer. Ray Kroc, a milk-shake machine salesman, bought the McDonald's restaurant concept from the McDonald brothers and turned it into one of the world's largest restaurant chains. Steve Jobs and his associates created the Macintosh computer, iPod, iPhone, and most recently, the iPad. J. K. Rowling was a welfare mom who has become one of the world's best storytellers. Then there's Oprah, a phenomenon. To say the odds of success were against her is a profound understatement, but she became a billionaire.

All these people, whose stories are well known, acquired wealth. But not everyone can do what they did, and many want to do things other than start a business, invent a product, or become a celebrity.

Peyton Manning, Brett Favre, LeBron James, Phil Mickelson, Venus and Serena Williams, Nancy Lopez, and scores of other professional athletes are millionaires. From humble beginnings, they turned their athletic talents into millions. Actually, for many of these superstars, product endorsements generate much more income than sports. Bruce Willis, Arnold Schwarzenegger, Angelina Jolie, Jim Carrey, Alan Jackson, Mariah Carey, Matt Damon, and a host of others who entertain us are millionaires. George Lucas made millions of dollars producing the Star Wars saga. Ozzy Osbourne makes millions being Ozzy. Stephen King, Tom Clancy, John Grisham, Nora Roberts, and Toni Morrison are multimillionaire writers. Anderson Cooper, Bill O'Reilly, and Katie Couric make millions while keeping the public informed. Larry King interviews scores of interesting people—we watch, and Larry makes millions.

Paris Hilton inherited wealth. Being an heiress is a sure way to millions. Howard Hughes started out with a lot of family money to work with and created even more wealth. Lottery and sweepstakes winners collect millions when they hit the jackpot. Jack Welch, the former CEO of General Electric, is a millionaire, and so are many other current and former CEOs. Many professionals acquire millions. Perhaps your doctor, or mine, is in the Millionaire's Club.

Many salespeople sell their way to riches. Selling anything from mundane items, such as pails and nails, to more mainstream products and services, such as cars, insurance, and real estate, to more sophisticated items, such as aircraft, consulting services, and investment banking, can put the proverbial peddler into the Millionaire's Club.

Entrepreneurs, business owners and many self-employed individuals acquire millionaire status through their business ventures. The founders of Starbucks, Amazon.com, Google, Quicken Loans, and hundreds of other businesses are millionaires.

Many investors have made millions in real estate, the stock market and other financial markets. Donald Trump made a fortune in real estate. Warren Buffett, the late John Templeton, Peter Lynch, and George Soros learned the business of investing and acquired vast wealth.

There are thousands of ordinary folks working regular mainstream jobs who have a seven-figure net worth. They accumulated it working for the right employer. Their retirement benefits and, in some cases, stock acquisition programs propelled them into the Millionaire's Club.

Some millionaires simply saved a million dollars or more during their working career. A diligent saver, given enough time and the magic of compounding, can enter the club.

Of the 309 million-plus people living in America, about 6 million people have cash, securities, and other financial assets worth a million dollars or more. About 20 million to 25 million more hold business and real estate assets worth a million dollars or more.

Millionaires are an interesting array of heirs, executives, celebrities, superstar athletes, entertainers, salespeople, entrepreneurs, business owners, investors, savers, unassuming low-profile neighbors, jackpot winners, professionals, and regular working people. Each has successfully traveled one of the twelve roads that lead to personal wealth.

The foregoing personal wealth numbers cited precede the economic collapse of 2008. It appears we've hit bottom and are on the way up again. Only time will tell. As of January 2010, there are probably fewer millionaires than there were in 2008. Some have lost their millions and they won't recover from the calamity. Others have seen their fortune shrink and they will have to wait for the value of their assets to recover. New millionaires will emerge from the economic calamity. So, despite a difficult economy, the number of millionaires will continue to grow throughout time.

The recent episode of economic woe is an occurrence we see every fifty to one hundred years. The book *Manias, Panics and Crashes, A History of Financial Crises* by Charles P. Kindleberger, Robert Aliber, and Robert Solow chronicles these economic downturns and explains many of the causes. The good news is we're improving the way we manage things and there are fewer of these events than in the past. The bad news is we don't know how to avoid them. Much of economics is theory and guesswork, and we don't have it all figured out yet. The best news is we'll recover. This too will pass, and there'll be economic prosperity again.

In fact, this is a time of great opportunity for some. Investors can buy businesses and assets cheaply. New businesses will emerge, and some will flourish. To quote Dickens, "It was the best of times; it was the worst of times....." Someday, we may look back and say the same thing about this era.

The aforementioned billionaires and millionaires all traveled a road that led to the Millionaire's Club. They successfully engaged in activities that created wealth. Are you on a road that leads to millions? We're free to embark on almost any of the roads that lead to riches, but some of these roads aren't accessible to everyone. For example, you might not be an heir or win the lottery. If you can't sing or dance, make people laugh, throw a football sixty yards or run a Fortune 500 company, you won't be able to take those routes. If you can't pass the entrance exam to medical or law school, you can't enter those professions. Nonetheless, there's plenty of opportunity.

The thing most millionaires have in common is their net worth. Beyond that, the similarities begin to vanish quickly. There are many books about the shared characteristics of successful people. There are many opinions and theories about personal success but no consensus about what it takes to acquire wealth. Different things work for different people. Many millionaires didn't start out with wealth in mind. It happened by accident or while they were doing something else. Sean Connery was advised to enter acting because he was handsome. He essentially shrugged his shoulders and said, "Why not?" He had no promising prospects or anything else to do, and before he knew it, he was 007 in *Her Majesty's Secret Service*. He simply needed a job and had no other prospects at the time.

Some fortunes were acquired by individuals determined to succeed. However, for many, the circumstances that brought personal wealth into their lives were the result of chance. A pharmacist invented Coca-Cola trying to invent a cough syrup. The Kellogg brothers were fooling around in their kitchen in Battle Creek, Michigan, and the corn flake was born. Laura

Ingles Wilder's daughter encouraged her to write down the *Little House on the Prairie* stories and have them published. She never dreamt they would make her wealthy and famous.

Whether by accident or on purpose, acquiring wealth and entering the Millionaire's Club is to your advantage. How do you do it? What's the secret?

THE TWELVE ROADS

Twelve roads lead to the Millionaire's Club. They're not a secret, having been well traveled. Stories, books, documentaries, and movies have been tracking these stories for years. Willy Loman, the tragic protagonist in Arthur Miller's classic stage drama *Death of a Salesman* talks to a vision of his deceased brother, who'd been a successful businessman, and asks, "What's the secret (to success)?" Willy died without learning the secret. He died a failure. His life was a classic tragedy, but part of the tragedy was that there was no secret.

The first thing you need to know about acquiring wealth is how wealthy people acquired their money. The answer goes back to the Getty quote about striking oil. Discovering oil, silver, gold, or diamonds can make you rich. Getting up early and working hard may help, but without the oil, you don't have the wealth. So, discovering and owning it is what made Getty rich. He could be characterized as an entrepreneur, investor, or executive. Each of those terms describes a person who's engaged in an activity that has the realistic potential to make him or her a millionaire.

Because getting from where you are now to the Millionaire's Club is a journey, these activities or endeavors that lead to wealth can be characterized as roads or routes. What roads did the wealthy travel on their way to millions?

Route 1:
Inherited wealth puts you on *Easy Street*. There's no travel required. You've already arrived and reside around the corner from the Millionaire's Club.

Route 2:
Lady Luck takes you down *The Yellow Brick Road*. This is where dreams come true. Buy a lottery ticket, roll the dice, spin the wheel, and bingo, you're a millionaire.

Route 3:
Professional sports can put you on the *Fast Track* to riches. A 95 mph fastball released from the left hand of a six-two pitcher is worth millions. So are scores of other talents that, collectively, make up the skill sets of professional athletes.

Route 4:
The *Street of Dreams* will take you from the footlights of Broadway to the bright lights of Hollywood. Many who entertain us earn a membership in the Millionaire's Club. After all, there's no business like show business!

Route 5:
Celebrities grab our attention and occupy our hearts and minds. They take *The Expressway to Your Heart* and acquire millions along the way.

Route 6:
A person who has a big job and flies first class on Executive Airways takes *The Jet Stream* to personal prosperity. He or she

enjoys dry martinis and gourmet meals, bonus miles, a pass to the executive lounge, and a black limo ride to the Millionaire's Club. Flight speed to riches is Mach 1.

Route 7:

The professions are *The Long Hard Road* to riches, but it's straight and wide. Those who hold professional status in society spend their lives working. Years of education and training, followed by long, hard days dealing with important and often critical matters can pay off handsomely. Professionals, such as doctors, lawyers, and accountants, command large fees for their services and can earn above-average wages. Professionals have an excellent chance of getting into the Millionaire's Club, and many do.

Route 8:

If you work on *Main Street, USA*, like the great majority of Americans who work for a living, don't lose heart. Traveling the same old road to and from work, day after day, can pay off if you work for the right employer. A regular job has made millionaires of many people. As long as you're working for the right company or organization, millionaire status may very well await you.

Route 9:

Few other occupations offer the upside potential and ease of entry as sales. The successful salesperson travels *Happy Trails* to big commissions, personal recognition, fabulous trips and prizes, no time clocks, and the respect and admiration of superiors and peers. A successful career in sales puts many in the Millionaire's Club.

Route 10:
Entrepreneurs invent new products or services, or even new industries or technologies. The successful ones become millionaires by engaging in private enterprise. Likewise, owning and operating a successful business is a ticket to millionaire status for many enterprising individuals. These people cruise along *Commerce Parkway* in pursuit of the big payoff, the proverbial home run. This is a difficult route, but for those who succeed, membership in the Millionaire's Club is certain.

Route 11:
Frugal living and diligent saving can put a thrifty person into the club. Thrift is a slow boat that follows the *Trade Winds* to wealth, but it travels a well-established route that's been navigated successfully for years. Financial security will almost certainly be realized by those who choose this route.

Route 12:
How can you move large numbers of people from where they are now to where they want to be in a busy, crowded society? *Public Transit!* You can ride sleek, underground cars and high-speed trains that whisk large numbers of people to the capital markets of the world and give them access to the remarkable world of personal investing. In the information age, more people will find the financial rewards they seek by traveling this route.

ROADS TO THE MILLIONAIRE'S CLUB:

You might think of another occupation or activity not mentioned above, but I submit, it will fit nicely into one of the categories listed.

These are the millionaires and the roads they traveled to acquire wealth. These routes aren't a secret, but on the other hand, they are unknown to many people. Those who want to succeed financially, create financial security, enjoy financial independence, and possess the happiness that personal prosperity provides, will need to successfully travel one or more of these roads.

Before we take a closer look at what route makes the most sense for you to travel there's another road I have not yet mentioned.

Route 13: *Back Roads to Prosperity.*
As G. Gordon Liddy once said, "Obviously crime pays, or there'd be no crime." Here are a few thoughts on ill-gotten money. Some acquire prosperity by lying, cheating, stealing, and by committing other crimes and misdemeanors. Others swindle, bamboozle, and use strong-arm tactics to take someone else's money. These are the back roads to wealth. Some of you may have thought about these routes already, not that you'd consider them for yourself. But what about those people who deal in drugs, prostitution, the illegal sale of alcohol, pornography, Ponzi scams, identity theft, gun running, the slave trade (it still exists), and countless other crimes against humanity and society? Don't forget corrupt Wall Street barons, corporate executives, and elected officials either. Boy, do they make money!

The depressing movie *Lord of War* is about the illegal sale of small arms. It was just a business to the gunrunner, who couldn't find any other business in which the margins were as good and the payoff so substantial. He ended up rich and, in a twisted way, pleased with his accomplishments. But he wasn't happy and lost his family. In the end, he was alone with his money.

Conning people out of their money to enrich oneself has been going on for thousands of years. There are hundreds of scams running in America every day. Some sharp operators, such as Bernard Madoff, con people—some of whom are particularly susceptible to these scams—out of their life savings. Madoff was a highly respected Wall Street investment manager who bilked thousands of starry-eyed investors out of billions of dollars over his career. Amazingly, these investors bought into the idea that in spite of the way the stock market moved, up or down, Madoff always made money. It was a fairy tale but people bought it. Those people are broke—or at least out enormous sums of money—and Madoff will spend the rest of his life in prison. His Ponzi scam is the biggest in history.

Newspapers throughout the country have been exposing predatory lending practices in the refinancing of home mortgages. Look what greed has done in the way of foreclosures and the sharp decline of home values. There are many ways to con people out of their money. Many sharp operators are clever and corrupt enough to enrich themselves at the cost of others, and it doesn't matter who they hurt—stockholders, taxpayers, employees, old ladies, children, or family.

When it comes to money, people can be ruthless. They'll steal in business or take things from others through legal maneuvering. They'll use their money, power, and contacts to destroy others, rationalizing they have a right to do so. Some will say, "It's just business."

Don't misunderstand my intentions. It would be naïve to write a serious book about becoming a millionaire without mentioning some fortunes have been acquired by less than honorable means. I don't advocate the illegal or immoral acquisition of wealth, but what I do and don't advocate doesn't matter to the unscrupulous among us.

I've worked with hundreds of small businesses throughout the years, and it isn't unusual to hear embezzlement stories when talking with business owners. Most of these thefts never make the newspapers, but there are millions of dollars stolen every year this way. Stealing, along with lying and cheating, has been a part of the human condition throughout history. It isn't likely to change anytime soon.

It's well worth noting, however, that morality plays an important role in the success of a society and economy, not to mention in our individual lives. Adam Smith, the astute Scot who wrote *The Wealth of Nations*, was a Presbyterian minister and found the merchant class in society repulsive. There was so much chicanery among them Smith thought society would be better off without them. But he also saw the promise of capitalism in the marketplace. Despite the avarice of the merchant class, capitalism creates wealth for individuals and for a nation.

A lawless or corrupt society has little chance for long-term survival. The lawless Wild West, greatly romanticized in books and motion pictures, lasted only a short period. The good people of the west could not build a better world for themselves and their families amid lawlessness. So they cleaned up and established law and order.

The character of citizens matters. Morality and ethics count. Conscience, a sense of right and wrong, and a sense of fairness and fair play contribute to the health of the nation. There will always be those who cheat and steal their way to a fortune, and they'll become members of the Millionaire's Club too. Many of those folks won't break the law, but their methods will be corrupt, illicit, and immoral.

The good news is our society is one of laws, and we have a strong moral tradition ingrained into our culture. Hopefully, such values will continue to dominate our national character. Humankind is capable of good and evil, but people, for the most part, tend to be good. That's not only my take; people like Aristotle and Adam Smith had the same opinion. The popular book *Freakonomics* by Steven D. Levitt and Stephen J. Dubner cited a study that addressed honesty. It's a novel and fascinating study based on data that illustrates most people tend to be honest. Thank God. Levitt and Dubner also emphasize that people tend to act in their own self-interests and respond to both positive and negative incentives. In any case, honesty is still the best policy.

All that's required for membership in the Millionaire's Club is a net worth of $1 million or its equivalent income. Many of those who travel the back roads to financial success will get a membership card. They'll have all of the money they need for financial security and financial independence. They'll gain admiration and respect from some simply because they have money. They will have influence among some because money is powerful. Many will win honors for their charity even though their gift was acquired at the expense of others. An unfortunate reality is that life isn't always fair. Even those who are dishonest win praise and admiration. It is ordained; the sun rises and sets on the just and unjust.

CHAPTER 3
LONG SHOT / BEST SHOT

Chance favors the prepared mind.
— **Louis Pasteur**

It's time to consider which of the twelve roads are accessible to you and which ones you can travel successfully.

INHERITED WEALTH (EASY STREET):

We have little control over whether we're born or marry into a wealthy family, but if that's the case, we're almost certain to become millionaires. Inheriting millions is the ultimate no-brainer. Keeping it is a challenge, but that's another matter.

At some point in their youths, people born into prosperous families realize they're members of a wealthy family and will be wealthy too someday. They'll inherit a fortune or at least benefit from it. The route to the Millionaire's Club for such people is birth, and their lifetime address is Easy Street. Many millionaires in America inherited their wealth.

There's little doubt that quality of life, financial security, and financial independence require the acquisition of a reasonable amount of wealth; inherited wealth is a gift, not the result of individual initiative. It still counts. It will provide an above-average, if not opulent, standard of living. But under these circumstances, there may be more of a risk it'll contribute to sadness and misery.

Barbara Hutton was the heiress to the Woolworth fortune. *Poor Little Rich Girl* was a movie about her tragic life. Doris Duke, heiress to the American Tobacco fortune, had an equally sad life story. Wealth deprived both of love and happiness. Similarly, Christina Onassis lived like royalty because of inherited wealth from her father. She died before she was forty, leaving her young daughter without a mother. An idle life with wealth is a risky proposition.

It's not that women have cornered personal tragedy. Countless tragic stories about men never find their way into print or movies. These are stories of people who were born to privilege but lived miserable lives despite their personal wealth. For that reason, many wealthy families take great care to ensure heirs responsibly use the wealth they inherit. Wealthy parents and grandparents are no different than parents and grandparents in general. They want the best for their children and grandchildren. Those who have wealth want it to contribute to the happiness and well-being, not detriment, of their heirs.

Yet there are other heirs who, likewise, never have to worry about money. They enjoy the money they've inherited and live happy productive lives. Many of these people look at wealth as an opportunity and regard it as a tool to do good. Thousands of charities, foundations, religious organizations and well-intentioned causes benefit from this wealth. These people devote time and energy to help others and to improve the world. Bill and Melinda Gates and Warren Buffett teamed up to make the Bill and Melinda Gates Foundation the biggest philanthropy in the world. The Kennedys and the Bushes are families who've devoted themselves to public service. There are people of all political persuasions who are in a position to devote themselves to public service. If you don't have to work, you can do what you want. Hopefully, it's something worthwhile.

One also could marry into wealth. Presumably, this would be done for love, not money, but sometimes it's for the money. One might become a millionaire in this way or at least reap many of the benefits of being so closely associated with wealth.

Sometimes a person becomes a millionaire because he or she is a beneficiary. Such a person could be the beneficiary of a trust or insurance policy of a million dollars or more. In some cases, the beneficiary may have had little, if anything, to do with becoming a beneficiary. In other cases, the beneficiary may have had a direct influence on creating the arrangement that resulted in receiving this money. A nonworking spouse may influence a working spouse, who's the breadwinner, to purchase life insurance to protect the family from poverty if the working spouse dies.

Others find their way into the Millionaire's Club through legal settlements or awards. It may be business related or have to do with defective products, personal injury or, in the worst case, a wrongful death. Such matters are never pleasant and, in some cases, they're tragic. Nonetheless, millions of dollars change hands yearly this way. Most of these issues involve much smaller sums of money, but there are substantial awards as well.

To some extent, this is a cosmic game over which we have little or no control. If you're not born into it, if you don't marry into it, if you're not adopted into it, or if you're not a beneficiary to it, this route to wealth is closed to you.

LUCK (THE YELLOW BRICK ROAD):

Every week, people throughout the country play the lottery hoping their ticket is one that gets them into the Millionaire's Club. Although there are big winners, the odds of winning the big games are anywhere from 1 in 35 million to 1 in 135 million. It's more likely you'll be struck by lightning several times before your ticket will be pulled to win one of these big jackpots. Only a handful of big winners are selected each year. But those who win are instant millionaires. For most people, gambling and gaming are forms of entertainment. It's fun and exciting, but it's always a long shot. Luck is The Yellow Brick Road, but the Emerald City is a fairy tale, a dream. The Wizard is a figment of the imagination. When Dorothy and her friends reached Oz, they didn't find what they were seeking. In the end, it was all a dream.

You may have seen the movie *A Civil Action*, which is based on a true story. A successful personal injury attorney reluctantly agrees to represent a number of families who've lost children in a strange series of mysterious deaths. This case costs his firm a considerable sum of money and his partners are trying to stay afloat. One partner spends the last of their cash buying instant lottery tickets in a desperate attempt to stay solvent. He doesn't win, and neither do most people who wager. For most people, gambling and wagering are entertainment. It's fun, as long as it doesn't become an addiction, but it isn't a ticket to financial security for the vast majority of us.

There are business organizations that "know the math" and have substantial sums of money available to make bets on a large number of games throughout the world. Many of these organizations thrive on gambling. This is speculation. It's a business. A typical individual isn't likely to have the same outcome. Some speculators become millionaires, but the downside of speculation is losing big.

Wagering isn't the only place you can be lucky. You might get a break in business or in your career. Another person may marry into wealth. Luck is something mysterious. Science can't explain it, and mathematics can't prove or disprove it, but somehow it seems to be a phenomenon some people experience. Hence the old expression, "I'll take luck over brains any day."

PROFESSIONAL SPORTS (THE FAST TRACK):

Many people are athletic, but only a few have the level of skill required to compete professionally. Sports have been a fascination of humankind since the beginning of civilization. It's a significant worldwide business, and those who are good enough to play at the professional level are paid handsomely. Even in games that don't generate billions in revenue, many players make above-average wages. If you're in the middle of the pack, you'll receive millions for your services, and if you're on top of your game, you'll become a multimillionaire.

But, there's only so much room in professional sports. The skill level requirements are so demanding only the best play. Few of us will ever put on a professional sports uniform. Big league sports isn't a route large numbers of us can travel successfully.

ENTERTAINMENT AND MEDIA (THE STREET OF DREAMS):

Likewise, some talented people will make it big in the entertainment field, but most people don't have the kind of talent it takes to make the big time. Arts and entertainment, like sports, have been a part of the human condition since the beginning of civilization. Music, books, movies, plays, musicals, and visual art are part of the entertainment industry. Those who create art and entertainment have an opportunity to become millionaires. If you can sing or dance, make people laugh, play Hamlet, or write a best-selling book or touching music, you may find your path ends at the Millionaire's Club. But again, not all talented people make it into the footlights. In fact, most talented people don't make it. Luck often is the element that makes a person a superstar, while another talent languishes in obscurity.

CELEBRITY (THE EXPRESSWAY TO YOUR HEART):

You can refer to famous athletes and entertainers as celebrities, but there's another group of people who are neither athletic nor artistic, but nonetheless, are celebrities. People such as retired military generals Norman Schwarzkopf and Tommy Franks, former presidents such as Bill Clinton and George W. Bush, or Miss America casualty Carrie Michelle Prejean are high-profile people who capture the public's attention. The late Princess Diana was a celebrity phenomenon. We're interested in these people and their stories, and that interest designates them as celebrities. All that attention can be turned into a lot of money, and many celebrities become millionaires for that reason. Former Alaska Governor Sarah Palin, who has become a superstar celebrity, is an example.

Some celebrities become famous by accident. Joe the Plumber is a good example. Joe was standing on his front lawn in Toledo, Ohio, when then presidential candidate Barack Obama strolled by in campaign mode, with reporters, photographers, and camera crews in tow, and struck up a conversation with Joe. Joe in turn asked a few tough questions and the ensuing dialogue got Joe on national TV. He has since been invited to appear on TV and radio talk shows and to attend various political campaign rallies as a guest of honor. If Joe plays his cards right he'll become a celebrity.

It's possible to become a celebrity on purpose by being in the public eye via radio, television, or newspaper. Generate publicity, and the next thing you know, you'll be asked to speak at a PTA meeting or senior luncheon. Then it's on to trade shows and conventions. Before you know it, you'll be a professional speaker. Anyone who has a story to tell about personal tragedy or triumph can command an audience. If the story is good enough, if it chokes people up or brings joy or inspiration to them, you may have a career as a speaker. You can become a celebrity.

Former presidents, war heroes, athletes, entertainers, and victims of atrocities receive our attention and win our hearts. We want to know about these people; we want to know and be around them. Certainly, the Hollywood set receives this kind of attention. Even criminals become celebrities. John Gotti comes to mind. Wealthy people such as Bill Gates, Oprah Winfrey, and Paris Hilton are celebrities. Nancy Lopez and Phil Mickelson are celebrity golfers. Tim McGraw and Mariah Carey are celebrity singers. Brian Williams and Diane Sawyer are celebrity newscasters. Celebrities in one field can become celebrities in another. Donald Trump is a great example. He's a successful businessman who has a popular TV show, *The Apprentice*. Jack Welch is no longer the CEO of General Electric, but he's a high-profile celebrity commentator, author, and speaker.

However, celebrity status is a long shot too. Like entertainment, sports, and the lottery, most people won't find personal wealth traveling this road. That's not to say you shouldn't embark on one of these roads. If any of the aforementioned occupations is your dream, give it a shot. But for the vast majority of us, they're long shots.

A BIG JOB (THE JET STREAM):

Although route six, A Big Job, is available to more of us, only a few have what it takes to succeed at this level. There are Big Jobs in almost every sector of the economy—private industry, government and nonprofit—and they go to only a few. These people are usually well educated with a track record of accomplishment, and, in some cases, those who know enough of the right people. There simply isn't enough opportunity to create large numbers of new millionaires this way because there are not enough Big Jobs.

That's not to say you shouldn't give it a shot if this is what you want to do and you believe you're qualified. High-level jobs provide considerable compensation packages that can make you a millionaire in no time.

Almost every CEO of a public company is a millionaire. So are many of the other officers and employees in large organizations. In these positions, you end up a millionaire even if you fail and get fired.

Is this something you can do? Some people start out with a high-level executive job as a goal and never achieve it. Others start out in a field just looking to get ahead and end up in a top spot. There may be a little luck involved too. There are a limited number of high-level executive jobs available, but most of us don't have the education, credentials, experience, skill, know-how, or contacts to land the ones available. It is very competitive at the top.

Many executives of public companies are in their forties or early fifties when they land a highly compensated job. They've spent the past fifteen to twenty years moving up the corporate ladder, honing their skills, and building an impressive list of accomplishments. A typical executive will make a million dollars or more in one year. Many times, such a person is paid a million dollars or more in cash compensation and many more millions in stock compensation. Sometimes it's hundreds of millions of dollars a year. That's a quick route to millions!

But not many of us will be running a Fortune 500 company, coaching a Big Ten college team, or directing a prime-time TV show anytime soon. The folks who end up here have been educated at some of the finest schools in the country. Many have graduate degrees, and some have accounting and law degrees—they're well-educated, bright people. Occasionally, you run across an executive who came up through the ranks and didn't attend college. Interestingly, eight out of the ten wealthiest Americans didn't finish college, according to *Forbes Magazine*.

Not all big jobs pay millions of dollars each year. A big job is one that pays annual compensation of $100,000 or more year after year. This is well above average and it should allow the wage earner to support an above-average standard of living and save and invest enough money to attain millionaire status. Examples of six-figure big jobs include an investment banker with a Wall Street firm, a mutual fund manager, a public school superintendent in a major city, the coach of a professional sports team, and an assistant coach as well. Those who earn more than $100,000 a year are in the top 10 percent of all wage earners in the United States.

THE PROFESSIONS (THE LONG HARD ROAD):

Occupations, such as doctors, lawyers, certified public accountants, and engineers, require a great deal of education and training. Testing and licensing also are required before you can work in these fields. The knowledge, skill, and expertise levels are higher than in most other occupations. We rely on people who hold professional status in society for our welfare and well-being. These people attend school for years and spend thousands of dollars—in some cases more than $100,000— on their education. They incur debt to become professionals. These professionals typically work long hours, and their work is often 24/7.

Those who have the talent and intelligence to attend such schools and enter one of the professions, such as medicine or law, are likely to become millionaires. Not every doctor, lawyer, CPA, engineer, or architect becomes a millionaire, but many do. Professional compensation usually is well above average. These people make enough money to live well and have enough to set aside for retirement. Many become financially independent. Accumulating millions of dollars of net worth during their working career isn't unusual for this group.

But becoming a professional isn't easy. These professionals are smart, earn high marks in school, and score well on difficult tests. If you have the brains and a passion for medicine, law, engineering, or architecture then being a professional is your likely route to a million-dollar net worth—it's not a long shot. However, most of us need to travel a different road.

THE RIGHT EMPLOYER (MAIN STREET):

If you work on Main Street for The Right Employer, you can become wealthy simply by being an employee of that company. Some of these employers want a long-term relationship with their employees and reward them with generous compensation and benefits. The Right Employer also may give employees opportunities to own, directly or indirectly, stock in the company. If the company succeeds over time and share values increase, employees win on several fronts: in many cases, they earn better-than-average wages, enough to live well; they have comprehensive benefits that provide short and long-term financial security; and owning company stock could make them financially independent.

Unfortunately, the right employer is getting more difficult to find. One of the unfortunate consequences of globalization, increased productivity, and the current recession is a substantial displacement of workers in our economy. Many of the new jobs being created don't provide a generous, overall compensation and benefits package. On the other hand, many new jobs being created are with employers that want to enrich the lives of employees. For thousands of us, working for the right employer is the road to millionaire status. This route deserves more attention. So we'll discuss it in more detail later. Because most of us work as employees, it only makes sense to work for a great employer.

SALES (HAPPY TRAILS):

If you can sell, you can travel Happy Trails to the Millionaire's Club. The good news is the field of sales is wide open. Almost anyone who wants to sell can find a company willing to give him or her a chance. The bad news is not everyone can sell. It isn't for everyone. If you can't sell, you'll become frustrated and disillusioned. If you can this may be your ticket to prosperity. Because sales is an opportunity for large numbers of people to succeed, we need to give this road serious consideration.

PRIVATE ENTERPRISE (COMMERCE PARKWAY):

Commerce Parkway is Route 10. Successful business ventures and business ownership are expressways to the Millionaire's Club. Successful business activities create large numbers of new millionaires in every generation. But business is a dangerous proposition for the unprepared or faint of heart. Like selling, there are few barriers to entry—anyone can start a business. But if you don't operate profitably, you'll fail, so you have to carefully examine the opportunities and the pitfalls on this route. We'll take a closer look at Commerce Parkway shortly.

THRIFT (THE TRADE WINDS):

Thrift follows the Trade Winds and is a slow boat to wealth. It's a well-established route. Spending carefully and always saving some of what you earn could be your ticket into the Millionaire's Club. Some of those anonymous neighbors, who are profiled in the book *The Millionaire Next Door*, traveled this route. David Bach's book *The Automatic Millionaire* addresses this route too. There's no question careful spending, frugal living, and disciplined long-term saving and investing allow many to enter the club. It's a tedious route and a long journey, but it'll pay off if you stay the course. In America, however, fewer of us are taking this route because we're world-class spenders and consumers. Spending creates the biggest economy in the world, but there's little to nothing left over after all that spending. What's left over is a key concept we'll review in a later chapter.

If you want to acquire wealth and enjoy the security and independence it brings, thrift may be your ticket to millions. This isn't a long shot. Almost anyone can practice thrift, but too many of us neglect this route. We need to consider it seriously.

Unfortunately, thrift isn't the answer for many of the have-nots. They don't earn enough money to be thrifty. They can't save because all their income is required to fund their living expenses. These folks just get by. Before they can practice thrift, they need to get more education and generate more income. Some of the have-nots have made a quantum leap from poverty to the Millionaire's Club, but they're the exceptions. When the have-nots practice thrift, they don't get far. They start out with high hopes and good intentions but, because of low wages, make little progress. We'll discuss this in more detail in a later chapter.

PERSONAL INVESTING (PUBLIC TRANSIT):

Personal Investing, Public Transit, is Route 12 to the Millionaire's Club. Obviously, you need money to be an investor, and the more you have to invest, the better. But you can earn millions even by starting out with small sums of money. For many people, the best opportunity to invest today is through a 401(k) retirement plan. To participate in such a plan, you have to be employed by a company that offers one. It may be your ticket to millions. More than any other time in our history, personal investing is something the masses can do. But it takes know-how, and there are many ways to lose money as an investor. Nonetheless, this is a great route for anyone to consider taking because it's open to all.

So, which road are you on? Which is the best for you to travel? In the following chapters, I'll emphasize the five roads that are the best shots for most people. Routes 1 through 5 are long shots. The inherited wealth on Easy Street, the lucky people who win big jackpots along the Yellow Brick Road, the Fast Track professional athletes run to riches, the Street of Dreams that runs from Broadway through Nashville to Hollywood for superstar entertainers, and the Expressway to Your Heart where celebrities cash in on their fame—these aren't routes everyone can take. They're not long shots for certain people, but large numbers of us won't get from where we are today to the Millionaire's Club traveling those routes.

The Jet Stream, the exclusive route for those who have a Big Job and the Long Hard Road professionals travel to financial security and independence are routes that offer opportunity for those who can meet the high standards for qualification. High-level jobs and professional positions aren't available in abundance but they are available to those who can meet the requirements demanded of professionals and those who hold leadership positions.

There are just shy of one million doctors in America serving a population of 309 million people. At this ratio, there are many who believe we don't need any more doctors. We just need to replace those who retire. Many people argue we have far too many attorneys. However, there are shortages in public accounting and some areas of engineering. In all societies, professions represent only a small percentage of the overall population. High-level jobs are limited too, but that's not to say ambitious people shouldn't try to work their way to the top if that's what they want in life.

Routes 8 through 12 are the five routes that offer more opportunity for more people than any other. Working for the right employer, a successful career in sales, becoming a successful entrepreneur or business owner, diligently practicing thrift, and successful investing represent the roads to riches the vast majority of people can travel. Most people are familiar with these roads. Maybe you have an idea about which route makes the most sense for you. Maybe you're on the right road already. If not, what's your best shot?

CHAPTER 4

MAIN STREET—WORKING FOR THE RIGHT EMPLOYER

It's all in a day's work.
— An eighteenth-century saying

The first road on our best shot list is working a regular job on Main Street. Most people work there, and those who work for the right employer may earn a membership in the Millionaire's Club. The right employer is one that makes a considerable contribution to your financial security and independence. Liking your job and enjoying your work are important considerations, but if your employer isn't contributing to making you a millionaire, it isn't the right employer.

If you're going to work eight to ten hours or more a day for thirty years or more, it'd be nice if you like what you do. It's an added benefit if your job is fun, enjoyable, and fulfilling—but you really don't have to like it. Some people work a certain job because they're good at it and it pays well, but they don't love it. Generally, working for the right employer is satisfying if for no other reason than the financial rewards. This may be all the job satisfaction that's required for some people, particularly if it's a ticket to the Millionaire's Club.

ABOUT WORKING FOR THE RIGHT EMPLOYER

Some companies have a reputation for making their employees millionaires. It usually doesn't happen overnight, but it can happen quickly. Normally, throughout a working career with the right employer, employees enjoy financial security through competitive wages and benefit plans that protect them and their families. The employer provides retirement benefits and, perhaps, an opportunity to acquire ownership in the company. This happened to many employees at Microsoft. Proctor & Gamble, R. J. Reynolds, Coke, Cisco Systems, and 3M Company have similar reputations. Larger public companies have the resources to offer substantial benefits to employees, and many share these resources with employees as a matter of business practice.

Also, there are privately held and family businesses that are generous to their employees, but unlike their public company counterparts, these companies don't have the benefit of having large quantities of publicly traded stock to use as a reward in their benefit plans. However, a profitable business of any size can contribute to creating financial security for its employees.

People who work in the public sector, in government and civil service jobs, or for nonprofit organizations, are often rewarded with financial security too. Federal, state, county, and city employees, as well as many teachers and nurses, receive first-class employee benefits during their working careers and in retirement.

Union employees often are the beneficiaries of above-average wages and benefits that are bargained for by the labor union that represents them. United Auto Worker members, for example, enjoy some of the best compensation and benefit programs in the country. Typically, after thirty years of work, a UAW member gets a pension that pays him or her and his or her spouse an income for life.

The right employer means one that provides compensation and benefits that'll enable employees to acquire financial security at least and hopefully become financially independent. Some of these employees acquire a million-dollar net worth working in a main street job. Others may not acquire a million-dollar net worth but will become the equivalent millionaire and earn the income a million-dollar net worth would produce.

I recall a conversation I had with an individual who would fit the description of the anonymous millionaire described in the book *The Millionaire Next Door*. We were talking about financial literacy among schoolchildren, how kids learned about money and how more people could become millionaires. At one point he paused, with a look of serious contemplation on his face, and then he blurted out, "I'm a millionaire!" It was as though he had never thought about it before. As he considered his own financial situation, he acknowledged he had a net worth of more than a million dollars. He was in his mid-fifties and had worked in public employment his entire life. His wife also worked. Between the two, they were well above the million-dollar mark. They had acquired financial security and they were financially independent. They could have retired at that time, in their fifties, with no worries about money. Furthermore, they had raised and educated three children.

We all know people, or have heard stories about people, who worked at regular jobs and were able to retire and not worry about money. Many of these people retired before age sixty-five. I know a former schoolteacher in his mid-fifties who retired after thirty years of teaching in a public high school. If he works for wages now, he's doing it for fun. He doesn't need to work because he's financially secure. He's the equivalent millionaire. Another schoolteacher I know will retire in five years and have 88 percent of his wages replaced with his retirement income.

Wages may be higher in many private-sector jobs, but benefits are often more generous in the public sector. Federal employees do well. They earn enough to live well and their retirement and health care benefits are for life. Your trip to the Millionaire's Club may be no more complicated than finding the right job in the public sector.

Various publications, such as *Fortune* and *Forbes Magazine*, regularly publish lists of companies that have a reputation for being generous employers. Often, companies are listed based on employee surveys conducted by the publishing organization or some other third party. So it isn't the company saying, "This is a great place to work," it's the employees.

CHARACTERISTICS OF THE RIGHT EMPLOYER

Most employers are businesses, and businesses have to make a profit. Employers usually won't pay more in wages than the market requires, but some employers pay above-average compensation. When Henry Ford started his company, he paid production workers $5 a day, which was a high wage at the time. The $5-a-day wage was one of the factors that contributed to creating the middle class in America. Many employers that make a profit are willing to share that profit with employees. The Lincoln Electric Company in Cleveland has one of the most well-known profit-sharing plans in the world. Lincoln rarely has to advertise for employees; prospective employees are lined up at the door. Your profit-sharing bonus each year could be 50 percent or more of your entire year's wages.

Health care is a critical employee benefit. Historically, serious illness has caused more home foreclosures than any other factor. Many employers provide comprehensive health care for employees and their families. Even though an employee may have to contribute to offset the cost of a health-care plan, comprehensive health care is an important element to create financial security. Some employers, such as large companies and public employers, often continue health care for their retired employees. Health care is the most expensive employee benefit an employer will provide. But because of rising health-care costs, many companies are cutting back on health-care benefits or passing more of the cost on to employees. Yet profitable companies that value their employees work hard to make sure employees have world-class health care with limited out-of-pocket expense.

Disabilities also can play havoc with your financial security. Many employers address this risk by providing employees with short-term and long-term disability insurance. If you're unable to work because of illness or incapacity, this coverage will replace some of your income, usually enough to keep you afloat while you're healing. Without it, you could face personal bankruptcy.

Generous employers also provide a large number of other benefits including dental insurance, paid vacation, personal time off, flex hours, child care, elder care, wellness and employee assistance programs, expense and tuition reimbursement, life insurance, accident and travel insurance, and benefits for family members too. Employers provide all these benefits to attract and retain talented employees who contribute to the growth, profitability, and success of the business. These employers provide financial security for their employees and their families during employees' working years, and help employees prepare for retirement too.

After a working career, which historically is thirty to forty years, an employee usually is eligible for retirement benefits, and generous employers deliver here too. But before we get into retirement benefits, let's discuss length of employment.

Depending on the statistics, the average employee changes jobs every two to eight years. Business conditions change so rapidly those employers who once had a reputation for offering lifetime employment, such as IBM and AT&T, no longer do so. Employers who had a reputation for never laying off employees, even during bad economic times, are approaching extinction. Most businesses will cut their workforce to stay profitable if conditions require it. This is a necessary and inevitable reality in business, yet there are those exceptional employers that rarely lay anyone off or let any employee go.

Likewise, talented employees realize new opportunities are created regularly. Many working people find it's in their best interest to change jobs as a condition of increasing their income. This new generation of employees has been referred to as portfolio workers. They have a portfolio of education, experience, and skills that are marketable, and they circulate their portfolio among prospective employers regularly, looking for the next opportunity.

Changing jobs every few years means your employee benefits may be great at one employer and less comprehensive at another. It also means you may not be building retirement benefits as quickly as you might if you stayed with an employer long term. You never know for certain what to expect in the employment markets and whether staying put or moving on is the right thing to do. But spending a lifetime with one employer isn't the norm today. If you're working for a generous employer, leaving for what may appear to be greener pastures could be a big mistake. On the other hand, leaving a dead-end job with an employer that's not contributing to your acquisition of long-term financial security and independence makes all the sense in the world.

The principal benefits that'll get you into the Millionaire's Club are retirement plans and ownership opportunities. Basically, there are two types of employee retirement plans that are offered by an employer. One is a pension, which basically provides a lifetime income that an employee receives in retirement. These lifetime payments could be substantial. Although such benefits could equal the wages you earned during your working years, most employers simply can't afford to offer such a generous benefit. Most pensions replace a portion or percentage of the wages you earned during your working career. Like social security, these payments come in every month for life. Many of these pension payments are similar in amount to what social security will pay. A lifetime income is an outstanding benefit. The bad news is that fewer employers are offering pensions because they're an expensive benefit. But, despite the expense, a profitable company uses a pension to attract and retain valuable employees. Likewise, public-sector employees, such as federal and state government workers, some nonprofit employees, and many union employees receive pension benefits.

The second type of employee retirement plan is known as a profit-sharing plan, and the most popular type is a 401(k) plan. Profit sharing means the employer may be willing to share some of the profits with employees. Unlike a pension that has to be funded by the employer even if there's no profit, this type of plan isn't nearly as expensive for an employer. In this case, an employer will make deposits from profits to the plan from time to time, and either invest the fund for the benefit of employees or give employees the responsibility of investing the money as they see fit. When employees retire, they use the money in the fund for retirement.

In a 401(k) profit-sharing plan, the employer gives the employees an opportunity to save some of their own money by encouraging employees to make payroll deduction contributions of some of their own wages to the plan. In most 401(k) plans, these contributions aren't taxed. Then the employer may make two kinds of contributions to the plan for the benefit of employees. One is a matching contribution in which the employer, as a means of encouraging employees to save some of their own earnings, contributes a sum equal to what the employee contributes. If the employee contributes one dollar of his or her own pay to the plan, the employer matches it with another dollar. The law limits the amount of money employees and employers can contribute to these plans, but the limits are high. Most employees can contribute as much as they like, but employers usually don't match every dollar employees contribute. The matching contribution in the vast majority of companies is usually less than a-dollar-for-dollar match. For every dollar you contribute, your employer may contribute twenty-five or fifty cents up to a specified amount of your wages, such as 6 percent.

The second kind of contribution an employer can make is a discretionary contribution. It's divided proportionately among the employees. All of the funds deposited into the plan earn interest or are invested, and no taxes are assessed against these earnings. Taxes are paid only when the employee takes money out of the plan, usually at retirement. A 401(k) plan is one of the most effective wealth-accumulation programs available to employees. Throughout a working career, an employee, contributing a reasonable percentage of pay to the plan, somewhere between $5,000 and $7,500 per year, could realistically expect to accumulate a million dollars or more in a 401(k) plan alone.

A newer type of 401(k) plan is a Roth 401(k). The tax on deposits and distributions are different than the plan described above. Many employers offer both plans.

If you're a public employee or work for a nonprofit organization, you may have a 401(k) plan available to you too. Such employers offer other plans, such as 403(b) and 457 plans. All these tax-favorable, payroll-deduction savings plans are great opportunities to accumulate wealth. Smaller employers can also set up several IRA (Individual Retirement Account) arrangements that operate in a similar fashion to a 401(k) plan.

Generally, employers deposit cash to employee retirement plans, but employers are permitted to contribute their own stock too. In the case of publicly traded companies, this is an attractive option for the employer, who can keep cash for use in the business and contribute stock to the retirement plan. Assuming the company does well over time and the stock value increases, employees are rewarded with large account balances when they retire. On the other hand, if a company stock doesn't perform well, employees receive meager benefits. If a company were to fail, an employee may get nothing. That's what happened in the case of Enron, the Texas energy company that collapsed in 2000. The value of the stock fell from $90 per share to less than $1 per share losing $11 billion of value for shareholders. Many of those were employees who owned stock directly as well as in their retirement plan accounts. Enron was a spectacular catastrophe that brought financial ruin to thousands.

Nonetheless, there are employers like Proctor & Gamble who have funded their employee plans with company stock and employees have been richly rewarded at retirement. In most cases, such a retirement plan is only partially funded with employer stock. Sometimes, even where other investment options are available, an employee will decide to place a large percentage of invested money in employer stock for no other reason than familiarity and loyalty. This could be a big mistake.

An important rule of long-term investing of this type is diversification. The investor who places most or all of his or her money in one security is taking an enormous risk. This level of risk for the typical working person generally is too great where retirement assets are concerned.

Many generous employers offer a pension and a 401(k) profit-sharing plan. These, along with social security, can give you a net worth of a million dollars or more, or give you the income a million dollars or more would produce.

Many public companies offer employees an opportunity to acquire direct ownership in the company through a stock-bonus plan, stock options, or a stock-purchase plan. The hope is the price of the company stock will increase throughout time and reward employees with substantial gains.

Another type of profit-sharing plan that may be offered by an employer is an ESOP (Employee Stock Ownership Plan). Generally, the only investment an ESOP acquires and holds in the plan is the stock of the company that establishes the ESOP, the employer. There's no diversification. The basic idea of an ESOP is to give employees an indirect ownership stake in their employer company through the retirement plan. In theory, employees who participate in such a plan would benefit from the success of the company in much the same way any owner would benefit. Hopefully, they'd become rich. There are hundreds of ESOP plans offered by public and private companies. When the company performs well, employees are rewarded richly. When the company performs poorly, employees find there are only meager retirement benefits, or in the worst case, no retirement benefits at all.

Some employers offer employees an opportunity to purchase stock in the company at a discount or with no brokerage fees. Many companies allow stockholders to reinvest dividends free of charge. Other companies offer stock bonuses, options, and appreciation rights to some employees. The opportunity to acquire stock in a well-managed, profitable, and hopefully growing and successful company can put you into the Millionaire's Club.

Another characteristic of generous employers is training, which is of incredible value. The knowledge and skills you acquire through training may make you a valuable employee. You'll have that knowledge and those skills for life. That can make you an attractive employee to any number of other employers. Because training is expensive, some employers don't make a big investment in it. Generous employers do.

The right employer also provides excellent working conditions and works hard to accommodate the needs of employees, on and off the job. Providing valuable training and rewarding employees with competitive compensation, comprehensive employee benefits, generous retirement benefits, good working conditions, and stock ownership are characteristics of the right employer.

CHARACTERISTICS OF A GREAT EMPLOYEE

Generally, employers are looking for competent, dependable employees. It doesn't matter if the job pays minimum wage or CEO compensation. Whatever the job, the employer needs the employee to meet, and hopefully exceed, performance requirements. Employee productivity contributes materially to employer profitability.

Great employers want employees who get the job done effectively and efficiently, who contribute to the success and growth of the company, and who do their best work all the time. Well-paying jobs with the right employer aren't available to everyone. You need to be a good employee and should strive to become as valuable as you can.

In many jobs, value starts with education. The more education you have, the more valuable you become. Historically, the average person who has a college degree will earn $1 million dollars more over a working career than the average person who didn't go to college. An education is worth a lot of money.

Certain types of education lead to more rewards than others. Currently, there's a high demand for accountants and engineers. Entry-level compensation in these fields is well above average. The federal government also has a high demand for employees and it is recruiting rather aggressively. These positions usually require a college education. People with graduate and doctorate degrees command above-average compensation too.

Productivity in America is high. By many measures, we're the most productive country in the world. That's good for business and the economy in general. For the efficient and effective employee, this productivity should command competitive compensation, comprehensive benefits, and longevity on the job. But productivity also results in the loss of jobs. Productivity is one of the leading causes of job loss in the United States. It makes U.S. companies more competitive, but it creates casualties in the workforce. But if you're going to become a stellar employee, you need to be productive.

There's also a disturbing trend among workers who report a lot of job-related stress because of the demands placed on them by their employer. Many employees are required to accomplish more in less time, work additional hours to accomplish more, and do it with fewer resources. Yet many employees do what it takes to get the job done with little stress, loving their jobs and employers.

Knowing how to do your job effectively and efficiently and being reliable, dependable, and resourceful is what makes an employee valuable. The late management thinker and commentator Peter Drucker invented the idea of "knowledge workers," those people in a company who possess an in-depth, functional, and intimate knowledge of the business—its products and services, practices and processes, customers, capabilities, and limitations—and use that knowledge to operate the business successfully. According to Drucker this cumulative knowledge, possessed in the collective mind of the workers in the company, is the company's most valuable asset. Many valuable employees become masters at what they do. Mastery doesn't necessarily require a college education, but training and experience are prerequisites to mastery, which is acquired by the diligent development and application of knowledge and skills over time.

Some employees are more valuable than others. The contribution they make to the ongoing success of a business or other endeavor is substantial or even critical. Some refer to these people as key employees. Even though every effective worker is valuable, key employees could be priceless. They complete tasks other employees can't. Key people often receive special compensation and benefit plans that aren't available to other employees. Few people start out with a goal of becoming a key person. They just work hard at something that's particularly valuable to an employer. They do a particularly good job of it, they're noticed, and the rest seems to take care of itself.

What is it you'd like to master? Where do your interests lie? What are your talents? What's your passion? One school of thought is you should do what you like to do when it comes to making a living. If you enjoy your job, work should be satisfying and, theoretically, you should master it. In some cases, that's true. I've heard many people profess they love what they do. They couldn't imagine doing anything else. You hear this frequently from athletes and artists. Sam Walton loved retail. Lee Iacocca loved cars and the automotive business. Yet other masters provide a different account. George Soros is a successful investor. He's a billionaire. Soros once responded to a question about how much he liked what he did. He said he never professed to like it; he was just good at it. Author Tom Clancy once commented a book is something that's inside you that eats its way out. I can attest to that! There's frustration, discomfort and pain associated with writing a book. Clancy also is quick to say being a successful author pays well. Before he wrote for a living, he was an insurance salesman. I don't know how successful he was at that, but his success as an author is well known. Some firefighters join a fire department because they love the job. We were able to see the passion, dedication, and bravery of those first responders in the terrorist attacks on 9/11. Yet, many firefighters pursue this line of work because it's a job that pays well, provides generous benefits, and allows them time to pursue other personal and economic interests.

To make the most of working on Main Street in a regular job, you have to do something that's valuable to an employer. If you like what you do, great. If you don't like it, but you're good at it, that's great too. The key is to be valuable. A talented employee, in addition to the compensation, benefits, and ownership opportunities a great employer provides, can earn enough to pay for a comfortable standard of living with something left over to save. A valuable employee working for a great employer can acquire financial security and independence.

Great employees in almost any business can do well. Wal-Mart isn't a high-tech business, and it doesn't recruit from Ivy League colleges and universities. But a valuable employee at Wal-Mart can move up and do quite well.

As an additional point of interest, Tom Friedman provides insightful guidelines about what kind of skills will be most valuable among employees in a global economy in his book *The World is Flat*.

UPSIDE

If you believe the best, or perhaps the only, road for you to travel is working on Main Street in a mainstream job, you can become a millionaire if you work for the right employer.

If you become a particularly valuable employee, one who exercises mastery over important and critical work, your chances of entering the Millionaire's Club are even more likely.

By working as an employee you don't have to make an investment in the business, you don't have the responsibility of running the business and you don't have to deal with the myriad issues and problems that have to be addressed operating the company. You don't have to sell the company's products or services either. You just have to show up, do a good job, and at the end of the day you get to go home. You get paid on time, you get paid what you expect, and the company provides, or at least subsidizes, comprehensive employee benefits that give you and your family financial security. Not a bad deal.

Most of us are working people. There are any number of good reasons to choose employment instead of self-employment. Having a job and working for a living is an honorable and dignified way to live. Hopefully, our work will sustain us and reward us. But working for the wrong employer is like heading down a dead-end street. It serves the needs of the moment but there is no future in it. It goes nowhere.

DOWNSIDE

As I write this, we're in the midst of one of the worst economic downturns in history. By many measures, the United States hasn't seen anything this bad since the Great Depression. It has earned the title, the Great Recession. Unemployment has been rising and is in double digits in some places. In times like these, even top-ranked employers will be challenged to continue their generous practices. Those who want to work on Main Street now will find it to be a far more difficult road to travel. Opportunities are still there but there are not as many and they are harder to find.

In many industries and sectors, wages, benefit packages, and employee rewards are shrinking. When you work on Main Street, you risk investing years of employment with a company only to end up disappointed. You could become the victim of a midcareer reduction or elimination of benefits, or even the loss of your job. A bad economy could hurt a great employer, resulting in the loss of your job or a reduction in benefits. A well-paying job with a top-ranked employer can reward you with millionaire status, but the matter is almost entirely outside your control.

Finding the right employer may require moving to another part of the country or even out of the country. The grass may be greener somewhere else or it may only look greener. Once you arrive, moving may turn out to be a mistake. Many starry-eyed people have left home only to be disappointed and disillusioned. Pa Ingalls, for example, took his family west looking for a better life. He built a little house on the prairie. Although Laura Ingalls Wilder made him famous in the *Little House* books, he never succeeded and his dreams never came true. Relocation is a complex issue that has serious implications. But if there's limited opportunity at home, you may need to move to find prosperity. Are you willing to move to the big city or across the country to find the right employer? Would you travel outside the country to make your fortune? Is it worth it?

IS WORKING ON MAIN STREET YOUR BEST SHOT?

You may want to do certain types of work. Perhaps you want to be a journalist. You don't want to start a magazine or online newspaper, you just want to write. Maybe you want to be a zookeeper, fashion designer, or toolmaker. You might want to help people and work for a charity. Maybe you want to be a doctor, but you prefer to heal the poor in a free clinic. Ask yourself, "Will my employment with a particular employer contribute to making me a millionaire?" If not, you have to consider finding a new employer that will get you into the Millionaire's Club. If that does not work out then consider what other best shots are available to you.

Many employees end up losing their job with what started out as the right employer. During your employment, learn enough about what you do and the business to be valuable to another employer. Learn enough to start your own business. Some day you may be faced with the need to do one or the other. Many employees who've watched their retirement nest egg melt down as their once-great employer imploded were positioned well enough to survive the heat. If your financial fate is in the hands of someone else, you should have a contingency plan. You should have a notion of where you can go next if things don't work out.

For those of you who do identify the right employer and land a job, this could be the best road for you to travel to prosperity.

How to Succeed Working in a Regular Job on Main Street, USA:

- Make up your mind you're going to work only for a top-ranked employer, one that will contribute to creating financial security in your life and make you wealthy.
- Do your homework, and identify a generous employer. Identify several.

- Make it your business to get a job with a top-ranked employer. That may mean moving or getting a certain type of education or training. It may take some time and several attempts to be hired but, in the end, it's worth it.
- Become a valuable employee and develop expertise and mastery over important and critical work.
- Have a contingency plan. What will you do if things don't work out?

CHAPTER 5

HAPPY TRAILS—SALES

Nothing happens until someone sells something.
                                        – **Unknown**

The next best shot to consider is sales. Perhaps you're already in sales or are planning a sales career. Maybe it's something you've thought about or people have recommended. The upside potential in sales is spectacular. In terms of financial rewards, there may be no better job than being a high-performing salesperson. If you can sell successfully, this may be your best route to the Millionaire's Club.

So, why would anyone want to sell? Some look at sales with disdain, and others see selling as a last chance. Not everyone values the important role salespeople play in an organization.

There's an old axiom in sales, "Nothing happens until someone sells something." It's true; no business can survive long without customers and orders. Sometimes customers buy products and services without the assistance of a salesperson, but many goods and services have to be sold, and a salesperson is an indispensable link in their distribution. No business would incur the expense of hiring, training, and paying salespeople if they could do without them. Many products and services require the skill and expertise of an accomplished salesperson to get them to market. A business will do almost anything to give effective incentives and rewards to its salespeople.

But not every sales job has high income potential. Those that pay $100,000 or more each year, which is well above average, pay enough to allow one to live well and save enough to earn a membership in the Millionaire's Club.

Where are such positions? An independent financial planner has this kind of potential, and financial planning is a growing field that offers tremendous opportunity. Anyone interested in accumulating wealth should have a relationship with a financial planner. People need professional help with their financial affairs, and a smart financial planner is as important as a skilled doctor, lawyer, or CPA. A good financial planner helps his or her clients succeed and succeeds himself or herself by doing so.

ABOUT SELLING

For those who love selling, it can be quite rewarding, but it takes a lot to become a successful salesperson. To start with, there's a lot of attrition in sales. The life insurance industry is a perfect example. It loses about 85 percent of the salespeople it hires within the first five years. Only fifteen people out of a hundred are still in the business and making a living five years after they were hired. Insurance companies with the best retention may lose only seventy-five to eighty people per hundred recruited. Not every business is as difficult as the life insurance business, but those who make a go of it in insurance and financial services can do extraordinarily well.

Often, it comes down to matching a salesperson with the right product or service. A person with sales ability could do poorly selling one product or service only to discover he or she is successful selling something else. If things aren't going well with one product or service, it may be better to steer your sales talents in another direction.

If this is your first attempt at sales, find a company that'll provide initial sales training. Larger companies tend to be prepared to invest time and money into training rookies. If no training is available, you may want to seek it on your own. The Dale Carnegie Organization, which has been training salespeople for years, has a good reputation; but there are plenty of others you may want to consider. If there's an interesting sales opportunity but no training, you'll have to rely on your own native ability and instincts, so it could be difficult starting. You could fail quickly. Learning how to do what salespeople do is what initial sales training teaches. But getting beaten up as a rookie is a form of training too. One way or the other, you have to learn how to be a salesperson. Get formal training if you can; otherwise, it's trial and error and that can be brutal.

If you already have sales experience and you're looking for a better opportunity, basic training shouldn't be necessary. Look for a good match between your skills and the product or service for sale. It's always nice to like and believe in what you sell. If this is the case, you'll have more conviction, enthusiasm, and excitement when selling, which has a positive impact on the customer.

THE BASICS

Product knowledge is knowing enough about your product or service to talk about it intelligently to your customers. It gives you the ability to answer questions and address concerns customers may have. New salespeople struggle with this because they fear looking foolish and losing a sale because of their lack of product knowledge. Many companies aren't willing to make a big investment of time and money into training salespeople in this area. Considering the turnover rates in many sales organizations, businesses have a difficult time justifying a big training expenditure, so they leave it up to a salesperson to acquire this knowledge himself or herself. A salesperson needs to make it his or her business to acquire the required knowledge. Before an employer makes a big investment in training it wants to see if you can set up appointments, make sales presentations, and garner interest from prospects. It may be difficult to believe any company would ask a salesperson to sell without proper training, but believe it. Sales requires a lot of initiative.

Sometimes a company will team a rookie salesperson with a senior salesperson or a technician as a form of training. Some products and services are complex, and it may take years of working with them to become competent. In any case, you need to acquire enough knowledge to be able to talk intelligently about what you're selling.

Many people will tell you selling is simple. Their advice is to use the KISS method, "Keep it simple, stupid." Don't overcomplicate things; just simplify your sales presentation and keep making one sales call after another, asking for business. Sooner or later, someone will buy. This may be sound advice for products such as magazine subscriptions or vacuum cleaners, but it could be shortsighted for complex products. Some products can be sold using the KISS method but others require a more involved sales process.

I was a sales trainer and mentor for years. I worked with rookie salespeople and taught them how to sell a complex financial planning service to sophisticated customers. It took two to three years before these salespeople could work without my assistance. After that time, they no longer needed me because they had acquired the necessary knowledge and were competent.

If you enter sales, gain a solid knowledge of your products and services as quickly as you can, even if you have to do it on your own time. Or, as an alternative, form relationships with other people who can provide you or your customer with the necessary information. Customers aren't impressed if you can't answer their questions. The answer doesn't have to come from you, but it has to come from someone who knows his or her stuff.

Another consideration about sales is whether you want to sell something tangible or intangible. For example, cars are tangible, and auto insurance is intangible. Would you be more successful selling a tangible item such as a machine or an intangible item such as a financial service? For some salespeople, it doesn't matter; others might be better equipped to sell one rather than the other. There's no way to tell in advance. Some salespeople gravitate toward a certain product or learn through trial and error that they do better with one or the other.

Do you want to sell products and services that cost only a small amount or sell items that are more expensive? If you sell lower-priced items, you need high sales volume to succeed. Higher-priced items may take longer to sell, and although you don't need to sell as many to succeed, each sale is critical. You can't afford to be rejected too many times in big-ticket sales.

Another consideration is selling a product for which there's a lot of repeat business. For many products, once an initial sale is made, repeat sales follow. Anyone can see quickly the wisdom in selling a product or service that results in repeat business, but some sales positions don't offer that opportunity. Once you make a sale and you are paid, there's no repeat revenue. Office supplies would be an example of a business where repeat sales are the norm. In the insurance business, an agent generates repeat revenue from selling auto insurance policies where a renewal premium is due annually. Once you have an established list of customers, repeat sales are automatic. Of course, your product has to stay competitive and you have to keep your customers happy, which is where customer service comes in.

The other end of the spectrum is a situation in which the salesperson, once he or she sold something to a customer, has to go out and find another new customer to make another sale—there's no repeat business. At best, repeat sales with the same customer are spread throughout many years. You're always on the hunt for new customers. This is known as new-account selling, but it's a difficult road to travel. Many new account sales opportunities offer attractive incentives, rewards, and compensation. When a new account salesperson is effective, this kind of selling is quite rewarding. Selling computer mainframes, aircraft, software development, estate planning, and consulting services are examples of new account selling. Why would anyone want to sell big-ticket items like this and have to start the process over each time? Big-ticket items usually have big-ticket compensation associated with them. Big ticket selling is sometimes referred to as elephant hunting. All you have to do is shoot one elephant, and you can eat for a year. However, when you don't shoot the elephant, the situation becomes bleak. Yet some people excel at selling big-ticket items and thrive on the challenge.

Your best customer is another consideration. Do you want to sell to businesses or consumers? This is referred to as business-to-business (B to B) or business-to-consumer (B to C) sales. In some cases, the distinction is stated as wholesale vs. retail. Many retail sales jobs are rewarding but have limited income potential, while B-to-B sales work usually offers higher income potential. However, someone selling cars to consumers, which is retail, can make six figures or more a year, and a salesperson selling cleaning supplies to restaurants (B to B) may not do nearly as well.

Fundamentally, selling is a transaction between two parties—a salesperson and a customer. The principal medium through which this transaction takes place is communication. Salespeople talk to other people, so communication skills are important. Communication is a basic stimulus/response proposition. Someone says something, and another person listens (hopefully). One person explains something, and another person understands. Someone asks a question, and another answers. This kind of interaction is fundamental, but it's critical when selling. Knowing what to say and how to say it, what to ask and how to ask it, and listening to what the other party says in response are elementary skills in any thoughtful communication, especially in sales. A high-performing salesperson has to be a good talker and a better listener.

There's often a lot of telephone work involved in sales. Selling on the phone is called cold calling—some people refer to it as smiling and dialing or dialing for dollars. In any case, the telephone may be the gateway to your customers. This is difficult work with a lot of rejection. Many people can't do this and quickly develop call reluctance, which means you don't want to pick up the phone and make another call. It's a mild form of emotional trauma some people experience and never overcome. There are outstanding telephone sales training programs available for B-to-B and B-to-C sales for those who want to improve their telephone skills.

Some sales jobs are based completely on telemarketing. You never see the customer. Selling via the phone and never or seldom seeing a customer may work for you. But selling in this manner is difficult and, for some, impossible. If selling over the phone isn't for you, it doesn't mean you can't succeed in sales.

In pure telemarketing jobs, mastery of the telephone is required if you're going to succeed. In other cases, in which the initial contact with the customer is on the phone, you only have to sell him or her on the idea of seeing you. You only have to master asking for the appointment rather than selling a product or service. You sell face to face.

Some companies emphasize organizational skills. Salespeople generally are responsible for their own time and activity. Some believe well-organized salespeople make more sales, keep customers, and are more successful. In some companies, being organized is a part of the culture. However, there are successful salespeople who are hopelessly disorganized. Organized people look at their haphazard peers and marvel at how they sell anything. Some sales managers and trainers believe organizational skills are a must. They might not welcome a disorganized salesperson. For others, it's a secondary consideration, or of no importance at all, assuming the person can generate sales.

The late Sam Walton considered himself a merchandiser, and he was, but he had to do a lot of one-on-one selling as he built Wal-Mart into the world's largest retailer. Before Wal-Mart sold stock to the public, the company was desperate for cash. Sam spent much of his time pitching banks and insurance companies throughout the country to lend him more money to fuel the company's growth. This was a difficult sell, particularly considering the millions of dollars of debt the company was carrying. But Sam got the job done and proved to be an effective salesman even though he was one of the world's most disorganized people, according to his biographer.

Some industries have an organizational system that's unique to that industry. The One Card System is famous in the life insurance business and is touted as having made a material contribution to the success of thousands of agents. The one card system is a method of organizing contact activity using index cards. But most businesses today rely on third-party tools, such as a BlackBerry, for their sales staff. Organizational tools aren't likely to make you a successful salesperson, but they can help you accomplish the job effectively. To dismiss an opportunity to improve one's own productivity is foolish. Most salespeople have to work hard and smart. Wasting time is never a good idea, but being organized is.

However, it's easy to waste a lot of time in sales. Unlike production workers, many organizations leave salespeople to themselves to manage their day without supervision. Time management is critical, takes a lot of self-discipline, and is the undoing of many salespeople. Time management is a competency any good salesperson has to develop. Some sales organizations use technology to monitor what salespeople are doing with their time. Because so much business is being done over phones, computers, and the Internet, software has been developed to capture a salesperson's activity and calculate the time he or she is selling. These are effective management tools that make salespeople more accountable for their time. That's a good thing, even though it feels like Big Brother is watching. Remember, time is money.

The business environment has become casual in terms of people's dress, appearance, grooming, and manners. You don't have to make a fashion statement to succeed in sales, but an unkempt appearance makes a bad impression. Because the business world has become so casual, some companies have imposed dress codes again. If your company doesn't have guidelines, you can read books about dressing for success or listen to consultants and specialists who will counsel you on dress, color, grooming and, believe it or not, manners. Being ill mannered, or even crude, has become the norm among some people in society. Ladies and gentlemen may soon be on the endangered species list. A salesperson who presents himself or herself poorly puts himself or herself at a disadvantage. If looking professional is objectionable to you, at least be neutral. Poor dress and grooming turn people off and make you look ignorant. Crude and vulgar behavior turns many people off. A salesperson can't afford to make that kind of impression. Some salespeople get away with such behavior, but it's a bad practice.

Managing numbers is a significant part of sales, and some sales trainers emphasize this. All you have to do is make enough phone calls, visit enough people, and ask for the order enough times, and you'll be successful. This is good advice for some products and services. Almost every sales organization will analyze its numbers and publish information illustrating that if you follow the formula success is almost a certainty. Managing the numbers is the tedious part of selling. You have to make calls and visit people to succeed.

On the other hand, the proposition that sales is entirely a numbers game is shortsighted. If you say the wrong thing to potential customers time after time, you'll fail even if you manage the numbers.

A sales presentation usually is a standard set of information a salesperson relays to a prospect. A presentation may include visual materials to show the customer. Sales presentations, which may be scripted and rehearsed, differ from product to product and service to service but, at least for rookies, they are standardized. A veteran often customizes a standardized presentation to suit himself or herself. Sales managers hate this, but it's quite natural for you to adapt something to your own style. All baseball batters swing the bat, but there are numerous batting stances and swing patterns. Batters do what feels good and what works for them. So do successful salespeople. Making effective presentations is another competency a salesperson needs to possess to succeed.

Sales presentations usually end with a call to action. A salesperson asks a customer to do something that's a step closer to buying a product or service. This call to action is known as closing, where the rubber meets the road, as they say. If you're afraid to ask people to buy, you'll never succeed in sales. If you can't close successfully, your career in sales will be short lived. Some people find asking people to buy something objectionable. It seems rude and ill mannered to them. Sales isn't for them. Many salespeople are taught closing is a technique. It's like a golf swing. If you do it just right, the customer always says yes and gives you a check.

But not all customers buy because a salesperson used a particular technique. If it appears you're using a technique, it could backfire. People don't like being manipulated. Customers make a decision to buy or not for their own reasons. A sharp salesperson will influence the customer to make a decision in his or her favor and won't manipulate.

Often a customer says he or she needs to think about it, talk it over with his or her spouse, attorney, or business partner. The customer may ask for additional information or say he or she wants competitive quotes before making a decision. These are called objections.

Salespeople are trained to expect these objections and be prepared to deal with them. Like closing, some sales trainers teach salespeople to use various techniques to answer objections. Objections have to be answered, but if it's perceived to be manipulation, it could backfire. Objections sometimes arise because a salesperson didn't address particular issues in the presentation. They may occur because the customer hasn't arrived at a point where he or she is intellectually, psychologically, or emotionally ready to say yes. In many cases, the customer isn't the final decision maker. So, in some instances, answering objections may solve the problem and the sale can be closed. In other cases, answering objections with answers that pressure the customer may be futile. There's a danger a salesperson might offend or alienate a customer by persisting. Trying to force the customer to buy before he or she is ready could result in making no sale at all. Persisting in objection answering—no matter how clever the answer—can be perceived as pressure and it could alienate the customer. A successful salesperson learns how to answer objections with finesse and has the good judgment to know when to back off and give the customer time to sort things out.

The sale of some products and services happens over a short period. Selling discount coupons door-to-door or selling cookware at a home show are single-event sales presentations and take only a short period, maybe minutes. Other sales take a series of contacts or meetings and may take weeks or months to complete. Selling employee benefit programs to a business, or an automated mailing system to an insurance company or bank, can take a year. Following up and following through are competencies a salesperson needs here. Managing the sales process and making sure you meet the customer's needs and expectations are key ingredients in making the sale. Following up and following through are within your control. Your employer and the customer expect you to do a good job in this regard. To some extent, the amount of necessary follow-up will depend on the product or service you're selling. The competent salesperson will make this a priority and keep his or her customer happy with the attention.

Customer service is something that takes place after the sale is made. This is critical when repeat sales are desired. The sale of some products and services are one-time events and customer service is a nonissue. A vacuum cleaner salesperson is trained to sell the vacuum cleaner, period. Customer service is the manufacturer's responsibility.

Many sales training programs place an emphasis on relationship building. The belief is to sell your product and keep the customer over the long haul; a personal relationship has to be established. Some sales jobs require a salesperson spend some of his or her time schmoozing the customer.

Salespeople are almost universally ambitious, and they demonstrate perseverance. They're looking for a legitimate opportunity to succeed financially, and sales offers that opportunity. A strong work ethic is usually required in sales. Sales takes physical, emotional, and psychological stamina.

A positive mental attitude, enthusiasm, and a genuine excitement about what you're doing also may contribute to your success. Many consider goal setting a necessity if you are going to succeed as a salesperson. You'll hear a lot about goal setting if you become a salesperson.

There are many self-help books and training programs that address goal setting. I'm not convinced these books always deliver the desired results, but if it works for you, do it. Goal setting is simply a plan for success.

It's nice to like your work. Selling can be fun, exciting, and satisfying. I remember having a conversation with a high-performing salesperson about what was fun and exciting about selling. He decided it wasn't the satisfaction of making a sale and getting a new customer, or even the money he made—although all of those things were desirable and appreciated—it was the thrill of the hunt and the day-to-day engagement with prospects and customers in the marketplace that was fun. It was transitioning from a "no" to a "yes" that was a high. But some days you get beat up in the marketplace, and from time to time, you slide into a slump and need a shot of motivation or some rest and relaxation to get you back on track.

A salesperson has to master a number of competencies to succeed. Hopefully, the foregoing will give you some insight into the business of selling and help you decide if it's the road you should travel to wealth and prosperity. Now that we've covered the basics, let's take a closer look at successful selling.

BEYOND THE BASICS

All successful salespeople have one thing in common—they convince people to act or buy. How do they do it? In some cases, just applying the basics of selling will get the job done, but many sales are the result of other factors that go beyond the basics.

Many salespeople are likable. When customers are asked why they do business with a particular salesperson, they often respond that they just like the person. They say he's a nice guy or she's a real sweetheart to work with. Some salespeople are naturally likable—they don't do anything consciously to be likable. Perhaps it's personality or one of many different characteristics. In other cases, a salesperson consciously does things that will make him or her more likable. Dale Carnegie's book *How to Win Friends and Influence People* is all about what you can do to be liked.

Likeability is an intangible that tips the scale in favor of a salesperson. It's a form of influence. It's subtle. A customer may not even know he or she made a buying decision because of this influence. I've heard countless people confess they had no idea why they bought something. They say, "It seemed like a good idea at the time." The influences that caused them to buy were imperceptible.

Many factors influence people. It could be wit, charm, charisma, or physical attractiveness. It could be know-how. It may be the communications skills of the salesperson. But a person who possesses the ability to influence others has an excellent chance of succeeding in sales. Are you influential? Do people seem to follow your lead? Is it easy for you to get your way with people? Do you believe that you have enough insight into people that you know how to appeal to them in an effective way? Can you get them to buy your product or service simply because it is you asking them to do so?

If you can impress people, you possess another quality that helps some salespeople succeed. Sometimes it's the salesperson who impresses a customer. Other times the product, process, or presentation impresses a client. If the customer is impressed, he or she is more inclined to buy. Sometimes a salesperson isn't consciously doing anything to impress the customer. It's automatic. The salesperson is just impressive to begin with. In other cases, he or she is consciously working at impressing the customer. Some sales processes impress customers, and salespeople use these processes intentionally to improve their chance of success. Many salespeople work to become more impressive. They dress better, improve their communication skills, expand their technical expertise, and work on their social skills, or do whatever it takes for them to become more impressive. Likeable salespeople who become masters of influence and can impress customers will make more sales. This goes beyond the basics of selling. These factors separate a good salesperson from a great one.

The ability to influence and impress customers isn't taught in basic sales training programs. Many successful salespeople aren't aware they possess these abilities. They may have possessed these capabilities when they began to sell or subconsciously developed them through experience. I've talked to enough successful salespeople to know most of them have no clue why they're successful. They're just grateful they are.

Successful salespeople not only master the basics of selling, they learn what their powers of influence are and use them. Robert B. Cialdini's book, *Influence*, provides insight into the power of influence. Neil Rackham's book, *SPIN Selling*, is considered a classic book about the subject of selling. It demonstrates the power of effective communication in selling and explains how it influences the outcome.

Some people enter sales with a set of built-in assets and skills that help them influence and impress other people. As they gain more sales experience, they refine their abilities, skills and methods, and apply them successfully. If you're going to travel Happy Trails to the Millionaire's Club and sell your way to prosperity, you must be or become competent in the basics of selling and learn to influence and impress people.

UPSIDE

There are few barriers to a career in sales. Anyone who wants the chance can find an organization that will give him or her a chance. Many sales positions offer legitimate six-figure income opportunities in addition to many other perks, including trips to fun and interesting places. You may have the chance to play golf on some of the world's finest courses. You may receive free golf balls, shirts, sweaters, and jewelry and dine at the best restaurants in the world. You may have the chance to travel the world and enjoy resort living created for the rich and famous. Upscale shopping excursions and visits to spas can pamper and rejuvenate you. You might even be asked to be a speaker for the national sales convention. Rewards include prizes, bonuses, awards, and recognition. The more successful you are the more respect you get from management and peers and the less accountable you become for your time.

DOWNSIDE

Selling isn't for everyone. Salespeople have to put up with a lot of rejection. Prospects will hang up on a salesperson or throw him or her out of their office. Many people can't take that kind of treatment. The work can be tedious too. A salesperson usually is required to work alone and may not get much help. A salesperson can work for hours, weeks, or months and not progress. It can become discouraging and lonely. There are some who believe salespeople are only out for themselves and don't care about the customer. That attitude exists among some salespeople and tarnishes the image of sales. That image isn't representative of professional salespeople, but it causes some to dismiss sales as a career. Selling is hard work and it will test your emotional, psychological, and physical stamina.

IS SELLING FOR YOU?

I've known scores of successful salespeople who have some things in common. Most successful ones, but not all, have a way with people. They're generally confident and have high self-esteem. They're determined and dedicated. But there are as many, and probably more, different characteristics among them. They possess different levels of intelligence. Some exhibit excellent social skills and manners while others are crude and obnoxious. Some dress well and others have no sense of fashion whatsoever. Some know their business and products inside out; others fake it. There's a wide range of diversity, even within the same company.

There's no one personality or profile that defines a salesperson. There's no universal model. The best advice you can give a would-be salesperson is to give sales a shot. If you like the benefits it has to offer, you should give this field serious consideration. If you like the idea of being independent and not punching a time clock, give it a try or several tries. If you think it's the route for you, don't let others discourage you. I've seen unlikely people end up on top of the sales charts. No one would have bet on them, but they succeeded anyway.

Although this isn't intended to be complete, here's a list that describes a number of different kinds of people you tend to find in sales. Perhaps one of these profiles describes you.

The Conqueror is a salesperson with a strong personality, a leader—not obnoxious or overbearing but one who commands attention and respect. He or she is strong willed and has strong convictions. A sheer force of will and personality tends to give this person an edge in sales and other endeavors. Customers are overwhelmed by this type and tend to follow his or her lead. He or she is strong, control oriented, and autocratic. He or she leads, directs, and tends to tell customers what to do. And they do it. Some see this type as pushy, but people respect him or her enough to do what he or she says, including buy what he or she wants to sell them. This type is a dominating figure.

The Consultant is another type of salesperson who positions himself or herself as an adviser. He or she is a problem solver and helps customers accomplish their goals and objectives. Customers feel good about this salesperson's expertise and knowledge and are comfortable with his or her recommendations and results. They buy from the Consultant because he or she impresses them with his or her knowledge and professionalism. He or she is thorough and competent, which is reassuring to customers. If his or her advice is challenged, it stands up to scrutiny. This person is a professional who knows his or her business.

The Celebrity is a salesperson who has acquired some acclaim in another field. A former professional athlete can often make a go of it in sales simply because of who he or she is. These people often are still connected to their former field, and customers like that association. This gives the Celebrity an edge that other salespeople don't have. If you're a celebrity, sales could be the way to cash in on your fame. Many former baseball, football, and basketball players sell stocks and bonds or insurance, and many of them are manufacturer's representatives and car dealers.

The Good Guy is a likeable salesperson. His or her personal charm wins people over, and they're inclined to do business with him or her. This type is friendly, never pushy, and makes friends of his or her customers. He or she may be humorous as well. Humor goes a long way in any endeavor, including sales. When customers are quizzed about why they bought from this type, they say they like him or her.

The Socializer is an adept salesperson who makes customers his or her friends and sells a lot in social settings or in other non-business environments. This is a person who may use membership in a club as a means of acquiring customers. He or she may do a lot of volunteer and community service work. The likeability factor associated with the Good Guy and the Socializer is well known in the field of sales. Socializers also tend to know a lot of people, which makes the business of finding customers easier.

The Technician is a whiz at product or technical knowledge and a master at his or her trade. Customers are blown away by his or her expertise, know-how, and skills. Most of us are impressed by the work of a master, particularly if it has an impact on us. Technicians aren't necessarily social, and they're often introverted and quiet. They're more interested in products or processes. Some people marvel at how a technician can sell anything. But customers respect and depend on these people and wouldn't trust anyone else.

The Producer is a person who doesn't sell to get orders from customers. This is a person who has good relationships with established customers and provides good customer service on an ongoing basis. The Producer maintains and tries to enhance customer relationships for the purpose of keeping customers and making additional sales. Some Producers don't have much sales ability, but they sell repeatedly because of their excellent customer relations skills. The producer isn't suited for new account selling.

The All-Business type is someone who's serious and methodical and doesn't rely on personality, likeability, or technical prowess to sell. He or she may not even like his or her customers, or people in general, much. Selling is a business to this person. He or she works the system and knows the strengths and weaknesses of his or her product, the market for it, the competition, the prices, and all of the angles. He or she is a sharp operator who relies on the need or desire for his or her product to sell it. The goal is to make sales. If he or she makes friends with customers, that's secondary. What the customer needs or wants is only a detail in the transaction. He or she is a deal-maker who may use incentives and rewards as leverage to make sales. His or her primary concern is to make money.

You may find all these different types of people in the same company selling the same products or services. Some organizations prefer to have one particular type of person, rather than the others. But all of these types of people have one ability in common—they convince people to purchase products and services by mastering the basics and influencing and impressing people.

Happy Trails has been the road to the Millionaire's Club for thousands of successful salespeople. It may be your ticket to personal prosperity too.

HOW TO BECOME A SUCCESSFUL SALESPERSON:

- Assess your sales assets. What is it about you that would make you an effective salesperson? Are you likable? Impressive? Do people tend to buy your advice and follow your lead? Do you communicate well? If you have sales assets, then sales may be for you. If you don't posses them, can you acquire these assets through education, training, and self-improvement. Do you want to?

- Get a job selling and try it out. Do it part time if necessary. If one sales job doesn't work out, try another. Try selling different things. See if you like it. See if you are successful at it.

- Learn what it is that salespeople do. Take a training program and talk to successful salespeople about what they do and how they do it.

- Master the basics of selling then go beyond and learn to impress, persuade, and influence people as a means of selling your product or service.

CHAPTER 6

COMMERCE PARKWAY—PRIVATE ENTERPRISE

The business of America is business.

– Calvin Coolidge

A googol is a very large number. It's the number one followed by 100 zeros. Saying googol is easier than saying 10 duotrigintillion, which is the word that expresses this number. But when you spell googol, Google, you identify a company valued at more than $100 billion. Although insignificant compared to a googol, $100 billion is a lot of money. Not bad for a company that was started by two graduate students in a dormitory room in 1996.

Larry Page and Sergey Brin, the founders of Google, the Internet's No. 1 search engine, are both younger than forty, and each has a personal net worth of about $15 billion. These two didn't take the expressway to riches, they took a rocket ship.

Although their success is extraordinary, there have been thousands who've traveled the old and heavily traveled route of private enterprise-people such as Thomas Edison, Henry Ford, Andrew Carnegie, Sam Walton, Dave Thomas and Bill Gates. These people successfully navigated the twists and turns on this road and found their way to the Millionaire's Club. Most of the world's fortunes have been made in private enterprise by those who traveled Commerce Parkway.

Many use the word entrepreneur to identify such people. Entrepreneur refers to the enterprising person who's the creator of a new idea around which a business or new industry can be built.

Entrepreneurs create much of the new wealth created in every generation. Entrepreneurs have original ideas that are the basis for a new product or service, or perhaps a new industry altogether. If the idea catches on, wealth follows. These new ideas create wealth, not only for the people who conceive and develop them, but for thousands of others who become associated with the idea. Ultimately, society benefits from the successes of these entrepreneurs too.

Creating a new business and acquiring personal wealth as a consequence of its success is exciting, satisfying, and financially rewarding. But owning a successful business, even an established one in an established industry, can be rewarding too. You don't have to create a new industry or business to enjoy the rewards available on Commerce Parkway, and it doesn't take forty years to become a millionaire. Private enterprise is an expressway to wealth.

In the popular book *The Millionaire Next Door*, the authors point out there's a disproportionate number of entrepreneurs among America's millionaires. In other words, many of the millionaires in America are business owners; so pay attention because anyone can take this route.

ABOUT PRIVATE ENTERPRISE

Let's start by describing some of the approaches used to travel this route successfully. Inventors, innovators, researchers, theorists, visionaries, and plain old business-minded people think about and experiment with new and original ideas. Some of this thinking and experimentation leads to the development of new products and services, many of which become commercially viable and succeed. In some cases, the idea starts out with a noncommercial purpose, but someone sees a commercial application and exploits the idea.

Before the invention of xerography in 1938, people had to use carbon paper to make a copy of a document. Carbon paper was inefficient, messy, and usually permitted you to make only one copy at a time. Ultimately, this invention led to development of the Xerox machine and the formation of the Xerox Company. That led to the formation of many rival companies competing in the copy-machine market. This one idea launched a new commercial enterprise and industry. It brought wealth to a large number of people.

The Internet is a similar example. The idea of communicating from one computer to another was created by the military, then used by professors and researchers at universities. It was a way to share information. Today, it's called the Internet. A company like Cisco Systems that didn't even exist until 1984 is a thriving enterprise today. Cisco manufactures much of the actual equipment that is the Internet. Hundreds of personal fortunes have been acquired as a consequence.

Entrepreneurs are prime movers who start something new that didn't exist before. Great personal wealth is the reward for this kind of achievement.

Most new ideas conceived by entrepreneurs don't become commercially viable immediately. The idea is conceived, and experimentation may take place. Any number of people tinker with a new idea or technology until someone develops it into an affordable product that is needed by businesses, the military, or consumers.

Henry Ford didn't invent the automobile, but he saw the potential of the automobile and invented a way to produce cars in large quantities at a price large numbers of people could afford. He changed the world and made a personal fortune. He was the world's first billionaire. (Depending on which account you read, Ford or J. D. Rockefeller was the first billionaire.) Historically, the time lag between the introduction of a new idea and its commercial viability has been ten to fifteen years. However, that time span is shrinking. New technologies are getting to market at an accelerating rate. Furthermore, the creator of the idea isn't necessarily the person who benefits from it. There are countless examples of this.

Ray Kroc was a milk-shake machine salesman who made it his business to meet the McDonald brothers when they ordered an extraordinary number of milk-shake machines for their California hamburger restaurant. When Kroc saw their operation, he saw the future and bought their business. Today, McDonald's is one of the largest and most successful restaurant chains in the world, and Kroc, who's deceased, made a fortune.

But not everyone is an inventor, innovator, or visionary. Some people are just business minded. I recall a widow who stepped into her husband's business after his death and increased sales tenfold. He was a technician, and she was a businesswoman. Other people possess skills that would allow them to start a business. Paula Deen of the Cooking Network is a great cook. She gained restaurant experience, opened her own restaurant, and is a successful restauranteur in Savannah, Georgia. She's also a TV celebrity and cookbook author. If she weren't a great cook, she wouldn't be where she is today. Deen developed that skill, acquired the requisite know-how, and turned it into a successful business and career.

Some people want the rewards that come along with successful business ownership but think they don't have the right skills. That kind of thinking could be shortsighted because many successful business owners are people who have management or financial skills. I know accountants, attorneys, and doctors who've left their professions to run businesses. These professionals may not know how to weld steel parts together, but they understand the economics of running a successful business. They hire the people needed to make the business operate well.

When a new industry emerges, hundreds of other businesses come along to support it. The railroad industry created new opportunities in the hotel and resort business, and the airline industry created the car-rental business.

The first automobiles produced weren't the sophisticated machines we have now. Ford's Model T had to be hand cranked to start the engine. The electric starter motor, invented by two General Motors engineers, Charles Kettering and Clyde Coleman, eliminated the need for the hand crank. Windshield wipers and defoggers, anti-locking brakes and thousands of other improvements to the automobile have created one new business after another. Now, the same thing is happening with the computer, cell phone, and Internet.

There are more opportunities for entrepreneurs now than in the past. More than one hundred years ago, near the end of the industrial revolution in America, people thought there was nothing left to invent or discover. That was before the development of penicillin, atomic energy, rockets, fast food, the transistor, aviation, and the computer chip. Currently, there's more to discover and invent than ever before. The focus of our attention is different, but the opportunity is tremendous. As we look to the future, we see biotechnology, genetic engineering, nanotechnology, robotics, alternate sources of energy, fuel cell technology, commercial space travel, and all the needs that'll have to be filled because of longer life expectancy and higher standards of living.

In his book, *The Fortune at the Bottom of the Pyramid*, C. K. Prahalad (now deceased) identifies a huge market and opportunity among the have-nots of society, particularly the poorest of the poor. He points out that by setting conventional thinking aside, through innovation, businesses can be created among the poor to offer products and services on which they can make a profit. This isn't exploitation; rather, he's talking about financing tiny businesses that provide useful products and services sold at a fair price by poor people who are engaged in entrepreneurial activities. This is a profound insight that could lead many aspiring entrepreneurs into an untapped market. The world always has been, and continues to be, a fertile and exciting place for entrepreneurs.

In the future, successful business owners won't all operate a high-tech computer or Internet company. Fortunes will be made in these areas, but there will continue to be thousands of opportunities in low-tech areas too. People still need to live comfortably and safely. They need to be transported from one place to another. They want to be entertained, amused, and have good health and movie-star looks. They need to be warm in the winter and cool in the summer. Kids still need to go to school and play in sporting competitions. There's plenty of low-tech opportunity. The old axiom, "Find a need and fill it," is still the basis for creating a successful business. And I'd add to that: Find a want and fill it.

But businesses are often started with a product or service that isn't needed. People didn't need a television or a minivan. But they wanted to be entertained, and hauling the kids around town was much easier with a minivan. In some cases, the product creates the market.

Sometimes a person just says, "I've always wanted to own a restaurant. I just want to work for myself. I'll never get ahead working for someone else." These sentiments often lead the would-be entrepreneur or business owner onto this road. An enterprising person may not be filling an unsatisfied need or attempting to introduce a new product but simply wants to be a business owner, and owning and operating almost any kind of business will do. I recall the story of a former IBM employee who was given an early retirement package but felt he was too young to retire. He began to look for business opportunities and purchased a franchise. It was a discount haircut franchise. He wasn't a barber and never cut any hair, but he became a successful franchisee who owned a number of stores.

Many contemporary inventors are well educated and trained to do highly specialized work, such as engineering or research, which is often done for a company that employs the inventor; but many inventors use their education, training, and work experience to invent for themselves. Then they sell their ideas or start their own business. Some of you are inventors, and your ideas may be the basis for your business and fortune.

Henry Ford and Sam Walton were innovators. Ford created the assembly line and mass production. He made cars in large quantities and was able to sell them at low prices. Only the wealthy could afford an automobile before Ford came along, but the assembly line made cars affordable for the masses. Ford also introduced the $5-a-day wage, which was well above the wages paid in those days. Ford's innovations changed the world. What do you see that can be improved?

Walton saw other merchandisers build businesses around the idea of high volume and significant discounts. He studied their retailing strategies and improved them. His vision was to lower the cost of living for consumers. He endeavored to make Wal-Mart the lowest priced provider of merchandise in the country, and he succeeded. Walton made Wal-Mart the merchant of choice for millions of shoppers. Collectively, his heirs are among the wealthiest families in the world.

The Wright brothers experimented with manned flight. They were obsessed with the idea. They discovered how to make a machine fly. What's your obsession? What new industries and products are yet to be created? What is it we can't do that humankind wants to do or needs to do? Perhaps you see a way to clean up the environment, cure cancer, or become less dependent on imported oil.

Albert Einstein was a theorist whose theories changed the world. Einstein wasn't entrepreneurial, but his thinking launched the atomic energy age and industry. As a result, thousands of other businesses came along. Do you have ideas that are the basis for new businesses?

Leonardo da Vinci was a visionary genius and artist who saw the future. Centuries ago, he drew pictures of strange mechanical devices. One of those pictures closely resembles the automatic transmission that propels cars. Another was the helicopter.

An entrepreneur is a person who sees a new way of doing things, which leads to the creation of a new industry or product. He or she investigates and researches the idea. Ray Kroc was alert and intuitive enough to see the possibilities of the McDonald's fast-food concept. The Google guys were techies who saw the need for a better way to search the Internet. They saw a need and an opportunity and did something with both. What new ideas represent an opportunity that can be applied on a larger scale and make you a millionaire?

In other cases, enterprising individuals, knowing and appreciating the benefits of successful business ownership, decide to start their own business in an established industry. There's no new idea, but a would-be business owner believes there's opportunity and decides to take a chance. Many car washes and movie theaters are privately owned businesses. Paint manufacturers, beverage distributors, restaurants, and office supply businesses aren't new. A want-to-be business owner starts a new company in an established industry and believes he or she will succeed because he or she possesses the know-how to operate such a business; or he or she sees an opportunity in the marketplace he or she thinks he or she can exploit. Often, these new business owners worked in a particular industry as an employee and learned the business. By doing so, they acquired the know-how to run their own business.

Capital One Bank, which is a huge success story, is the brainchild of entrepreneurial thinking of two business consultants about an established business—the credit card. The co-founders of the company saw an opportunity to charge interest on credit cards based on individual credit risk. Rather than a one-size-fits-all credit card, they individualized the rate of interest based on credit scores and other criteria. Those with high credit scores receive lower rates, and those with poor credit scores pay a higher rate. This gave better credit risks a better deal and those with poor credit the opportunity to have a credit card and improve their credit score by making timely payments. This one idea was worth millions. What skills and know-how do you possess that you can use to own and operate your own business?

Among would-be business owners, there are those who prefer to purchase an established business. The risk of failure is greatly diminished because the business already is operating successfully, has customers, and is providing a product or service in demand.

Business ownership opportunities also exist in the form of dealerships, distributorships, and franchises. Historically, automobiles have been sold through dealers, who can't sell new cars without a contract with an auto manufacturer. Not everyone will qualify or have the connections to get a shot at owning a dealership. Those who qualify have a ready-made business to operate. There's no guarantee of success, and if you don't perform, you'll lose the dealership. But chances for success are substantially higher because the business model is refined; it's proven. And the principals, the auto manufacturers, make sure you have enough money to operate. They screen you for ability and help you avoid failure.

Many products get to market through a distributor, which is similar to a dealer. The manufacturer or producer of a product reaches the market through its distributors. If you have a chance to pick up a Budweiser distributorship in your town, do it. Distributors of all kinds do well financially.

Franchising is another business model used to get products to market. Most people are familiar with fast-food franchises such as McDonald's, Wendy's, and Subway. Hundreds of these opportunities are available all the time, with new ones offered each year. The basic concept of franchising is sound. The right franchise will put you into the Millionaire's Club.

Dealerships, distributorships, and franchises should be seriously considered by anyone who's looking for a legitimate business ownership opportunity. But you have to do your homework. Usually, you have to pay to play, and the cost of acquiring a franchise can be daunting. In some cases, financing is available, but not everyone qualifies.

Other entrepreneurial types start a business around an avocation or hobby. I read a news article about two sisters who were fitness advocates and started a business that taught employees how to work out at work—with the blessing of their employer—using common, everyday materials instead of expensive exercise equipment. A hobby or pastime may be the basis for starting your business.

While entrepreneurship and business ownership are challenging, history demonstrates that some people, such as immigrants, realize on their own or have it ingrained into them that business ownership is the only way to go. It's the fastest way to financial security and success. Many of these people would never consider another route. They know it may be difficult, and they realize the risk, but they also know there are few opportunities as great as private enterprise. They take this route despite the risk, demands, their limitations, and lack of resources. They take this road in any case because so much wealth can be created so quickly. The rewards for success in private enterprise can be astounding.

UPSIDE

Successful entrepreneurs or business owners have an excellent chance of becoming millionaires. They generally enjoy an above-average income, usually six figures or more; they have a seven-figure or eight-figure net worth, which gives them their membership in the Millionaire's Club; and they enjoy an above-average standard of living. According to the IRS, only 10 percent of taxpayers earn more than $90,000 a year. That puts successful business owners in the top 10 percent of income earners. These people typically enjoy their work and take pride in their achievements. They have a degree of prestige in the community and are financially independent. They're among the most financially successful people in the world.

DOWNSIDE

The risks are above average in business. Not every entrepreneur succeeds—many fail. Some fail many times but succeed in the end. Others succeed initially only to fail in the end. So, before you take a second mortgage on the house and max out ten credit cards for working capital, look at the numbers.

The majority of new business start-ups fail within five years. Some estimates are as high as 95 percent, in which case only 5 percent survive. These aren't positive numbers—odds are you'll fail. The biggest reason for new business failure is undercapitalization. The business doesn't have enough money to operate. In some cases, this results in the personal bankruptcy of an entrepreneur. Having your hopes and dreams dashed in this way isn't pleasant, but it's reality. Most people who start a business have no idea how much money will be required to succeed. In most cases, it's much more than anticipated.

Another reason new businesses fail is poor management. Those who don't get killed because of cash shortages get killed by making mistakes. They didn't know as much as they thought about operating a business. They didn't possess management, marketing, or financial skills, and it did them in. An entrepreneur may have a great idea but little to no business acumen and his or her business fails because of errors, mistakes, and ignorance.

And don't forget competition. If you have a good idea and can make it work, there are loads of other businesspeople who'll gladly compete with you. If they have more money than you, they can drive you right out of business in no time by undercutting your prices or distributing the product or service more efficiently. It's unlikely you'll be the only person trying to make a go of it in a particular type of business. There are plenty of competitors who want the same customers you're going after. In some cases, competitors are so well capitalized and managed, you can't compete. Mom-and-pop retail stores were no match for Wal-Mart.

Over time, some businesses become irrelevant. The market for the product or service simply goes away. The TV and appliance repair business is an example. You may be an expert at repair, but given the low cost of replacing such items, coupled with the addition of new features on new models, the repair business is vanishing. And then there's Murphy's law—"If anything can go wrong, it will." In business, things go wrong all the time. Sometimes, Murphy puts you out of business.

This is a difficult and potentially treacherous road to travel, but the ride is exhilarating, and the payoff is fabulous for those who succeed.

IS PRIVATE ENTERPRISE FOR YOU?

Entrepreneurs and business owners are risk takers. There are countless mishaps and failures among those who take this route. There's no guarantee, and the odds are against you. How's that for motivation? Don't be foolish, but don't be afraid. The payoff can be so substantial, it's worth some risk.

Take your time, and do your homework. There are countless books, magazines, newsletters, and Web sites devoted to helping entrepreneurs succeed. Entrepreneurial studies are offered as accredited courses at universities throughout the country. State and federal agencies, such as the Small Business Administration and your state's Department of Economic Development, promote and assist entrepreneurs. There's a lot of help and assistance available.

One thing that's valuable and may be required is a business plan. Creating a business plan will force you to think about numerous aspects of operating a business you might otherwise overlook. It'll help you determine how much money you need to invest in the business or have available to operate without running out of cash. Excellent software is available for creating a business plan. It's a useful tool, and it can go a long way to help you get started. If creating a business plan is intimidating, there are support groups available at local organizations such as your local community college.

Venture capitalists, as well as other people who evaluate businesses and business ventures, take a serious look at who'll be running a new business before they invest. In the view of many of these people, everything depends on the skill, know-how, and, most importantly, the determination of the operator. If they like the business idea and are sold on the operator, they invest. If you're entrepreneurial but not a businessperson or don't understand marketing or finance, get help or a partner. You need to be honest with yourself. You have to be a solid operator.

Another piece of advice often given to new business owners is to engage the services of a business attorney and accountant who specialize in working with small businesses. Although professional services aren't cheap, such advice may prove to be priceless.

Take your time, and do your homework. Smart businesspeople typically aren't impulsive—they're thoughtful and careful. You'll have to work long, difficult hours, and your business will become your life.

Many successful entrepreneurs and business owners never started out with wealth as their goal. Money wasn't what motivated them to pursue their interests or start a business. Perhaps curiosity, a passionate interest in something, the need to work without supervision, or any number of other personal drivers led them to their own businesses. Some simply lost their job and needed to make a living. Money and wealth were simply byproducts of their efforts.

While business ownership is one of the best roads to personal wealth, choosing this route for the sake of riches alone may be a mistake. Successful business owners are excited about their businesses. It's their life, at least while they're building it. They also pay attention to details. Successful business owners are hands-on people and tend to know their business inside out, from top to bottom. The little things can be your competitive advantage or your Achilles heel. Passionate business owners keep their eye on the store. They may not be good at everything, such as marketing or finance, but they have a keen awareness of what makes the business a success, and they manage it carefully.

How'd you like to become a millionaire early in your lifetime and enjoy financial independence sooner rather than later? A lifetime of financial independence is the reward for the successful entrepreneur and business owner. There are few barriers to entry, and almost anyone can be enterprising. Are you entrepreneurial, an innovator, a theorist, or a visionary? Are you a businessperson? Do you have a keen sense for business and how one operates? Can you acquire the requisite business skills? Have you learned enough about what you do for a living to start your own business? Is there a dealership, distributorship, or franchise for you? You need to be a risk taker, but wealth is the reward and worth the risk for many. Wealth awaits those who can avoid the hazards encountered on Commerce Parkway, those who can successfully navigate the treacherous twists and turns along the way.

HOW TO SUCCEED AT PRIVATE ENTERPRISE:

- Determine if you have the appetite, resources, and disposition to work on your own without the safety of a regular paycheck.
- Given the high odds for failure and the low odds for success, determine if you're willing to take the risk. Can you afford to do so? Is it worth risking your credit rating and personal bankruptcy if you fail? Can your family tolerate the risk, long hours, discouragement, and disappointment that may come?

- If you're not a businessperson, find a partner who is. You may be a great entrepreneur with wonderful ideas, but if you don't know how to run a business, you're likely to fail. Find the help you need.
- Create a realistic business plan, and determine how much money you need, then double it. You should probably triple it. Then figure out how you can acquire the money you need. This will be a challenge, but one you'll have to address. You have to have enough money to operate until you become profitable. Once a business is up and running, it can finance itself, but you'll need seed money to get started.
- Ideally, there should be a form of household income to pay the bills while you're getting started. Without such an income, the stress levels will rise significantly. Anticipate that it will take longer than you expect to get your business up and running.
- Be prepared for things to go wrong or not to go as you expect. Be prepared to address these issues because your success, perhaps even your survival, will depend on your ability to analyze and correct problems.
- Discuss going into business and the kind of business you're considering with knowledgeable people before you jump. You might want to avoid advice from friends and relatives. In most cases, they are not qualified to give advice about business and they are not objective because of the close relationship. It's easy to be naive about the competitiveness of the marketplace and the harsh realities of business. You want to feel reasonably confident you know what you're getting into and can handle it.
- Continue to learn all you can about business in general.

CHAPTER 7

THE TRADE WINDS—THRIFT

A penny saved is a penny earned.
— Benjamin Franklin

The advice provided in this chapter is simple to state, easy to understand, and, it would seem, nearly impossible to follow: save a portion of every dollar you earn or acquire. Pay yourself first by putting money into savings and investment arrangements before you pay for anything else. Never spend what you save. This is your treasure, your wealth.

Be thrifty, live within your means, never spend more than you earn, and spend successfully. A successful spender seldom pays top dollar for goods and services. He or she gets the most for his or her money and buys what he or she wants, but pays less to get it.

The ancient proverb, "Waste not, want not," and Ben Franklin's wisdom, stated above, have been passed along from generation to generation. We hear it, we say it makes sense, but too many of us don't do it. Intellectually, it makes sense; but emotionally and psychologically, it may not. We make more decisions and choices because of what's going on in our gut rather than our head. Being thrifty has become the road not taken. Despite the fact it's one of the surest paths to financial security, instant gratification and pleasure have replaced a desire for self-reliance. Spending almost everything to pay for a higher standard of living at the expense of accumulating wealth has become the norm, and saving for the future and being prepared for a rainy day has become passé. But because this is one of the surest paths to prosperity, give this route serious consideration.

ABOUT THRIFT

Thrifty people don't resent being serious about saving and careful about spending. They feel good about it and don't feel deprived. Spending everything they earn and living today on tomorrow's income is just plain dumb in their view. They don't relate to people who do such things. It's not known for sure how thrifty people acquire this behavior, but it serves them well.

Some acquire thrifty habits from family members or friends. Others get it from positive and negative experiences. For some, it seems to be instinctive or a matter of personality. Some acquire it in school; many get it from difficult times. Those who suffered through the Great Depression never forgot their pain, and most were careful with their money thereafter. No one seems to know for sure what it takes to make a person thrifty.

I know a thrifty young married woman with two young children who moonlights from time to time to make a few extra bucks. She saves regularly and is careful about how she spends money. She waits to buy items until she has the cash to pay for them. She doesn't use credit to acquire what she wants. I've known her for many years and have closely observed her habits. One day, I asked her how she had become so thrifty. After some thought, she said her parents never gave her money. They provided her with all of life's necessities, but she had to work for money to buy what she wanted including clothes, movie and concert tickets, and automobile insurance when she began to drive. She had to pay for gasoline too. There were no handouts or freebies. As far back as she could remember, when she wanted something, she had to pay for it herself. Her attitude is money comes only from your hard work. Therefore, you must get the most out of every expenditure. Furthermore, she doesn't believe anyone will rescue her if she runs out of money. She saves diligently with the expectation the unexpected happens all the time. She knows she has to be self-reliant, and she's somewhat fearful of not having money if she really needs it for something.

I've never seen a compelling study about how thrifty behavior and attitudes are developed, nor am I aware of a consensus about how to instill thrift in a person. Those who've suffered the pain of poverty may be thriftier than others. Parents can play a big role instilling this into their children, but parents love to indulge their children. It's much easier than disciplining them and a lot more fun. It's easy for a child to develop a sense of privilege and entitlement. Consequently, many children never develop a strong work ethic and self-reliance.

Thrift is an important and essential value we've lost sight of in America. Thrift, even in small quantities, is essential for most individuals to enjoy any economic success. The very wealthy don't need to be thrifty because they're not going to run out of money. At one point, Ted Turner, the founder of CNN, saw his net worth decline from more than $10 billion to less than $1 billion. He had only a few hundred million left but could still buy whatever he needed. For the vast majority of us, a 90 percent decline in net worth would completely screw up our standard of living, but it didn't bother Turner all that much.

Earlier, I mentioned that Thomas Jefferson once commented about the need for everyone to have a modest amount of personal prosperity to be happy. Ironically, Jefferson lived most of his life well beyond his means. He had substantial amounts of debt and died broke. Jefferson is a giant figure, not only in American history, but world history too. He was a man of great and lofty ideas, and few people in history could state such ideas so eloquently. He was brilliant by many standards. He also liked the good life and wasn't willing to forgo the finer things in life. He provided himself, his family, and friends with the best of everything. Jefferson must have worried about money and had problems with his creditors, which is unpleasant and nerve-racking, but he managed to make it through life without his house of cards collapsing. He died deep in debt, and his assets, consisting principally of his Monticello estate, were insufficient to satisfy his creditors.

I have clients who would tell me this is a great story: "Hey, if it's good enough for Thomas Jefferson, it's good enough for me." Many of them chose to live like Jefferson, on the edge. Some succeeded, others didn't. Too much credit personally, in society or in business is a time bomb. Look at the mess the United States and the world are in today. The country and planet are reeling from a financial catastrophe of gargantuan proportions. Western economies and citizens have been, among other things, on an extended credit binge, and now we have to pay the price for the excess. When things blow up like this, the effects are devastating.

Too many people have no interest in saving and are compelled by powerful desires to spend and consume. Critics are quick to admonish the thinking, behavior, attitude, values, and character of those of us who aren't thrifty. All you have to do is pay yourself first. Live within your means. Buy only on sale. This kind of advice suggests it's a simple choice any reasonable person with character and discipline would make. In fact, many commentators take the position wealth is a choice. You simply decide wealth is something you want, and you do what's necessary to get it. It's that simple. But it really isn't.

Implying a person is stupid or has poor character doesn't usually elicit change in that person. Few things, except intense desire and severe trauma, change people. But telling people they're screwed up won't work. There's much more to consumer behavior than intellect and character. The NOVA documentary *Mind Over Money* that aired on PBS in April 2010 provided some interesting insight into this phenomenon.

Some people are uneducated when it comes to money. Ignorance about money matters can be costly, hence the familiar phrase "A fool and his money are soon parted." But the issue extends beyond ignorance. We still have a great deal to learn about the role our emotions and psyche play in our behavior and decision making. Why do we do things that aren't in our best interest? Why do we act foolishly and make shortsighted decisions? Why don't we make smart decisions when it comes to money?

When you ask people these questions, they simply don't know why. But something is at the root of our behavior. In many instances, it's a matter of what makes us feel good. We make decisions based on what provides us pleasure. There's scientific evidence a shopping spree results in the release of brain chemicals that create a sense of euphoria and satisfaction. Business and academic researchers are studying consumer behavior and what's behind it. There are studies under way at universities throughout the country designed to give us a better understanding of ourselves and why we do the things we do. It won't be long before we have new insight, fresh theories, and better tools to help us diagnose behavior and help modify those that are undesirable and troublesome. Until those breakthroughs are available, we're left to consider who can travel this route successfully and who needs to head in a different direction.

The genuinely thrifty person can travel this route successfully. Thrifty people save regularly and steadily accumulate wealth over time. They spend carefully. Their lifestyle is usually modest, and they demonstrate at least some frugal behavior. Some keep everything they've ever owned—they don't throw anything away. They have a conservative attitude toward money. They appreciate that money is difficult to come by and easy to consume, so they make expenditures only after careful consideration. Furthermore, they tend not to make impulse purchases. They buy thoughtfully and shop around for a good deal. They distinguish between a need and a want, and then they buy what they need and avoid purchasing what they want.

Other people sometimes see these folks as cheap. And perhaps they are. In a business or retail transaction, we tend to think of a provider of goods or services as cheap when he or she delivers less than expected or promised. In social settings, a cheap person fails to pay his or her share for something or excessively borrows from others to satisfy his or her own needs. Socially, being cheap is sometimes equated with being ill mannered and impolite. In some cases, a frugal person ends up being cheap because of his or her compelling desire to hang on to his or her money. But cheap and frugal aren't synonymous. Many frugal people have a keen sense of fairness in business and the good manners to be gracious and generous in a social setting.

John Bogle, the founder and former CEO of the Vanguard Group of Mutual Funds is famously frugal. (Vanguard is on the Fortune 500 list of best places to work in 2006—The Right Employer). Bogle recognized that if an investor could keep the cost of investing down, he would make more money. Bogle founded Vanguard on that premise. The Vanguard Index 500 fund replicates the performance of the S&P 500 stock market index. The fund has no manager because money is invested in a fixed set of 500 stocks. There's no trading, so there's no need to incur trading costs, which saves investors in the fund a lot of money. Many people subscribe to this approach to investing, which has made Vanguard one of the more successful mutual fund companies in the country.

But Bogle didn't stop there. He ran a tight ship and made sure he was exemplary. He made his own travel plans and always insisted on the best airline fare available and a discount for his hotel room. He shopped until he received a discount. Then he made sure as many employees as possible heard about his success. That's not being cheap, it's being smart. The success of Vanguard and Bogle is directly related to thoughtful, careful spending.

Is thrift alone enough? My guess is Bogle would say yes. Remember, however, the qualification for membership in the

Millionaire's Club is a million-dollar net worth or its equivalent income. What does it take to save your way into the Millionaire's Club?

Consider savings that earn interest, such as bank deposits. Let's further assume a would-be future millionaire is currently age twenty-five, and has forty years to accomplish his or her goal. It would take savings of $846.05 each month for forty years, earning 4 percent interest compounded monthly, to accumulate a million dollars. That works out to $28.20 every day, assuming an average thirty-day month, or $42.30 per workday, considering there are twenty workdays in a month. Not everyone can save this much, but many can. The average hourly wage, based on information provided by the U.S. Department of Labor Web site, is just shy of $14.00 per hour. The average wage earner would have to commit the first sixty-one hours of work each month to set aside $846.05 every month. Sixty-one hours of wages represent 38 percent of monthly income. Most working people can't save this much each month, but the thrifty wage earners would find a way do it. Above-average wage earners will find it much easier to save this sum.

The minimum wage is $7.30 per hour in Ohio, and the minimum-wage worker would have almost nothing left to live on if he or she were willing to save the required sum after taxes. So this approach isn't possible for most low-wage workers. Minimum-wage and low-wage workers have to increase their wages or find another route to prosperity. Amazingly, you'll find that rare saver who, despite income limitations, will sacrifice to accomplish his or her goal. Such a person will work two or three jobs if necessary.

DINK (Duel Income, No Kids) is an acronym that describes a couple with two incomes and no children in a household.

When two spouses are working and there are no child-related expenditures, saving is easy. In many such households, DINKs live on one income and save the other. Some DINKs retire in their forties. But most people want children and have two on average. In terms of entering the Millionaire's Club, DINKs have an advantage over those who raise families. But a thrifty person will find a way to save what's required to accumulate wealth.

Many two-income households raising families find they too can save the requisite amount and acquire a million dollars or more. But relying on the interest paid on deposit type accounts to accumulate wealth takes time and discipline, and there's little room for error. The numbers are inflexible. At 4 percent, you need to save $846.05 every month for forty years. If you have more time, great. For those who can save more money each month, the goal is easier to achieve. If you achieve a return higher than 4 percent, you can get it done with less money. If you have a lump sum to start—perhaps from an inheritance, settlement, tax refund, or bonus—and add it to your savings, the desired outcome will be easier to achieve.

If you save $846.05 every month for forty years, you'll have saved $406,104. The difference between what you saved and the $1,000,000 you've accumulated is $596,896 in interest, the money you've earned by letting bankers and lenders use your money. Saving this way to accumulate wealth has been going on for years.

Many financial advisers and commentators recommend that you save 10 to 15 percent of wages for long-term purposes, such as retirement. A person willing to set aside 15 percent a month would have to earn monthly wages of $5,640.34 each month to save the desired $846.05. That's an annual income of $67,684. Referring back to chapter one, you will recall this income is slightly above the median income for a four-member household. Certainly, some households can save $846.05 each month but, for many, this would be an ambitious sum. In the next chapter, I'll talk about how you can supercharge your saving and get to your goal with less fuel.

For people who have considerably less than forty years to accumulate a million dollars, this route becomes much more difficult. If you have only twenty years to accumulate a million dollars and you earn 4 percent interest on savings, you'd have to save $2,726.47 a month. Most people can't do this. Compound interest works its magic over long periods, so taking this route is more realistic for those who start young and stick with it.

A traveler who isn't thrifty can take this route to riches if he or she can change his or her ways and adopt thrifty behaviors. Some people change once they see the light. They change their ways, set a goal, and stick to it. Is a membership in the Millionaire's Club worth having? Is it worth working for? Is it worth sacrifice? For some people, a little sacrifice today for more happiness in the future makes sense. These people will do what's necessary to achieve it.

You have to be thrifty; otherwise, this isn't the route for you. Good intentions are useless without the correct actions. For those consumers who can change their ways and become thrifty, a membership in the club is possible.

It's appropriate to mention some of the positions people take who oppose thrift. I recall a woman in a seminar I was conducting who objected to the notion people should strive to acquire a million dollars or more during their lifetime. She thought living for today was more of a priority. "Why should I forgo happiness today? I could die tomorrow," she said. If you're going to die tomorrow, you don't need to save any money. But the problem with "eat, drink, and be merry because tomorrow you may die" is, as Dorothy Parker, said, "… you usually don't." Most people, about 83 percent, barring a bird flu pandemic or a nuclear calamity, will live beyond age sixty-five. But her comment is indicative of the resistance many people have to forgoing pleasure today in favor of a more secure future. It's not fun and doesn't feel good. It doesn't make sense to some.

Many people feel a life of sacrifice isn't worth it. They believe living well now is living right. Thomas Jefferson must have felt this way. This view isn't without merit. If being thrifty makes you unhappy, and sacrificing satisfaction today is too high a price to pay for financial security in the future, thrift isn't the route to riches for you. So hopefully, there's another road you can travel successfully.

Those who squander their income and assets aren't likely to enter the Millionaire's Club; and if they do, they may not be members very long. Insecurity is their likely fate. These people will have to spend a lifetime working for a living, assuming they remain healthy and work is available to them; otherwise, they'll have to depend on luck, the generosity of others, and programs such as Social Security, Medicare, Medicaid or welfare. There are countless stories of once wealthy entertainers, professional athletes, lottery winners, heirs, and heiresses who ended up broke. There'll be others in the future. Those who don't have a thrifty bone in their body or who feel being frugal is for other people need to find another way to enter the Millionaire's Club.

Some choose to live above their means and don't practice thrift as a matter of choice. It may not be a conscious choice, but it's a choice. These people are foregoing long-term financial security as a condition of living better today. Thrift is deferred happiness—you forego some happiness today to ensure happiness in the future. There are those who, knowingly, are taking a chance and betting something else will come along to provide them with the financial security they'll need in the future.

Being thrifty consists of spending less than you earn and saving enough to create financial security and independence in your life. As a means of finding enough dollars to save, thrift also means when you spend you get a lot for your money. It means you buy on sale, get discounts, don't buy pricey or premium products or services, and, in some cases, don't spend at all because you can't afford to or you just don't need to. It means using credit only when necessary and using it only to acquire an asset, such as a home. Sliding into debt for consumption is a bad idea. Using credit for entertainment and vacations isn't thrifty behavior. But a lot of consumer behavior is driven by emotion not intellect. That's why credit cards have been so successful and why credit card companies are so profitable. Put purchasing power into the hands of consumers, and they'll spend even if they don't have the money to cover the credit card bills at the end of the month. Credit cards are almost a necessity in the world we live in, and most cardholders use their credit cards responsibly. For those who don't, they pay in the form of higher interest charges, fees and poor credit scores. I know people who don't have a credit card by choice because they don't want the temptation.

If you have enough income and you have accumulated enough wealth, you can spend to your heart's delight. Spending for pleasure won't hurt you financially, but saving comes first and spending is second. This rule applies to almost everyone including those with big jobs, such as CEOs, professionals, or anyone else with above-average personal income and wealth.

Being cheap and hoarding money at the expense of reasonable happiness is foolish. Money is a means to an end, not an end itself, and the end you're looking for is financial security and independence. There are always two things you do with the money and assets you acquire—save some and spend some, in that order.

Those who can save 10 to 15 percent of wages or perhaps $500 every month during their working career can enter the Millionaire's Club. It may require sacrifice, but thrifty people are willing to do so. Being frugal will make the job of accumulating wealth that much easier. A few years ago, newspapers reported the story of a truck driver who gave a million dollars to his high school as a bequest from his estate. He had a humble job but saved and invested diligently during his lifetime. He lived in a modest house in a nice neighborhood and had a reputation for being frugal. He drove an old car and planted a vegetable garden each year to save on his grocery bill. He was the classic thrifty person and became a millionaire and philanthropist.

Another aspect of thrift is budgeting. Some thrifty people don't need a budget, but many do. Budgeting is an exercise one undertakes at the beginning of the year or month to estimate income and expenses. Start with an anticipated income. The budget allocates that income to cover expenses for the period. The first expenditure should be to savings. The balance can be used for expenses. Hopefully, there's additional money left over after expenditures that could be used for more saving or discretionary purchases (the things you want). The idea is that you can't exceed your budget; run your financial life like a businessperson runs his or her business. At the end of the month or year, review your budget and expenditures to determine if you're on or over budget. Examine and challenge your expenditures and look for places to save money. Look for places where money is leaking out of your budget and take steps to plug the leaks. You might be amazed to see how much money you spend on lunch. It might make you brown-bag it twice a week. You might realize you're withholding too much in payroll tax and you could increase your contribution to your 401(k) plan or a personal IRA. Be careful to stay on budget during the period.

I have a friend who was a world-class champion at budgeting. Her husband's regular paychecks were used to cover monthly expenses. At the end of each year she took her husband's annual bonus check and cashed it. Then she did her budget and allocated a portion of the cash to all of her anticipated expenditures. She put the budgeted sum for each expenditure, in cash, into an envelope that was labeled with the name of the expenditure. There was an envelope for yard maintenance, one for gifts, one for Christmas shopping, one for entertainment, and so on. She wouldn't spend more than she had in a particular envelope except in an emergency. If she had an unexpected expenditure, she might take money from another envelope such as entertainment. If the entertainment envelope ran dry, then it was Monopoly at the kitchen table for the rest of the year.

Not everyone can live on a budget, but everyone should try. Budgets are an essential part of running a successful business and are equally valuable for individuals and households.

UPSIDE

This route is a well-established road to riches. It has been well traveled. Reaching your destination is highly probable on this voyage if you stick to the course. If you're already thrifty, you're on your way. Keep it up. If you're not but can change and become thrifty, this may be your best bet for acquiring financial security and independence. Thrift isn't rocket science; most of us have the capacity for thrift. This route isn't exciting, but you know you'll reach your destination. As I've mentioned before, immigrants live out this story generation after generation. They come to America to get ahead and for a better life. They come to America, as well as other free and open societies, for freedom and opportunity, and they succeed. Immigrants tend to live inexpensively, work hard, work more than one job, spend carefully, and save. Generally, they take advantage of the opportunity. Those of us who are born here can succeed in a similar way.

DOWNSIDE

This is a long journey, which will take patience on your part. To succeed, it's best to start saving as early as possible. You must be disciplined and diligent. If you're not, you won't reach your destination. If spending and saving were simply matters of intellect, it'd be much easier to succeed. I recall a quote attributed to the famous Christian missionary, the late Albert Schweitzer. He was asked what was wrong with men today and said men simply don't think.

Why do some of us stand in line and pay $2 or more for a cup of coffee at Starbucks when we can get coffee faster at the drive-through window at McDonald's or Duncan Donuts for less than a buck? Some people say: "I deserve it," "It's a reward for working so hard," "I like the experience," "The service is so personalized," "The coffee is better," or "It's only a buck more." Ben Franklin would shudder at that. Some people would argue unless you have a highly developed pallet or you're a coffee connoisseur, the only difference is the price. It doesn't make sense to pay more, but we do it for reasons not driven by intellect. Repeat this behavior over a lifetime and it can cost you your financial security. Joni Mitchell sums up such behavior artistically in the lyrics of her song, *Help Me*: "doesn't it feel good...doesn't it feel goooood..."

Planning to save the same sum of money every month for forty years or more is a challenge. "The best laid plans of mice and men oft go awry," wrote John Steinbeck. It's almost certain that over such a time span your plans will be buffeted by chance, circumstance, and Murphy's law. Things change and go wrong, and there are many variables. You could lose your job and be out of work for an extended period. A family member or you could have a serious illness that consumes all your assets.

Interest rates are another issue. I used 4 percent in an earlier example, but as I write this, bank deposits are earning 1 to 3 percent. Throughout the past forty years, interest rates have risen above 16 percent and fallen to a low of below 1 percent. Although 4 percent is a reasonable long-term average, consistently making deposits at 4 percent is impossible. You'll have to recalculate and adjust to reach your goal. In a sense, you'd operate your savings plan much like a company operates a pension plan. You'd have to put your actuary's hat on from time to time to determine if you're ahead or behind your plan and adjust deposits accordingly. It works for pension plans; it can work for you too. It isn't automatic. You have to think about it, check on it, and work at it.

The two most important elements of thrift are attitude and discipline. You have to make up your mind you're going to be a prosperous person and do what's necessary to make that happen. You're not going to be deterred or defeated. You'll scorn foolish spending and relish saving. You have to make a plan and stick to it over a lifetime. There should be no exceptions. We should have a better attitude when it comes to accumulating wealth and becoming financially secure and independent. When obstacles present themselves, as they always do, we need to overcome them. When we get off track, we need to get back on it. When we lose heart, we need to double our resolve.

Our psyche and emotions are powerful drivers. They contribute mightily to our actions and inactions. Our decisions are determined in large part by these factors. If you suffered through the Great Depression or were poverty stricken sometime during your life, you might be a thrifty person because you don't want to feel that pain again.

If you want to get an up-close look at the pain and desperation that poverty brings, read Frank McCourt's book, *Angela's Ashes*, or see the movie. If you were ever hungry like McCourt was as a child, you'd never forget it, and you'd be careful to avoid that possibility for the rest of your life. On the other hand, if you were a ninety-pound weakling and were picked on as a kid, you might have a powerful drive to gain recognition and respect in life at any cost. You might be obsessed with landing a high-paying job, driving a $100,000 Mercedes, joining a prestigious country club, and wearing custom-made clothes at any cost.

IS THRIFT YOUR BEST SHOT?

Most fortunes in America weren't acquired by thrifty people, particularly large fortunes. But if you can't get there by any other route, this road is open to all. Thrifty people create financial security for themselves.

Frankly, anyone who wants to accumulate wealth and keep it needs to practice some thrift. Many millionaires end up spending all their money. If a successful salesperson doesn't save some of those big commissions, he or she won't enter the Millionaire's Club. If a wealthy doctor or architect spends everything on lavish living and spends more than he or she brings in, he or she will end up poor.

HOW TO BE THRIFTY:

- Earn as much as you can. Always look for ways to add to your earnings by earning raises, working overtime, part time, moonlighting, etc.

- Set aside a portion of your income (10 to 15 percent or more or a set sum, such as $500) every month. Set aside some of the assets you acquire too, such as gifts or an inheritance. These sums represent permanent savings. Permanent savings is money never spent. This is your accumulated wealth, and it'll provide you with the passive income you need to create financial security and independence.

- Create and live on a budget. Never spend more than you earn.

- Don't use credit cards for purchases you can't pay off at the end of the month.

- Live without personal debt. The only debt you should have is for a home mortgage.

- Try to buy used cars for cash. If you need a new car, look for the best deal on price and financing and try not to finance (or lease) for more than three years.

- Become a successful spender. Get the most for your money. Buy on sale, use coupons, and ask for discounts. Buy what you need and avoid what you want. Be frugal.

- Take full advantage of any employee benefit plans your employer may offer such as a 401(k) plan.

- Try to end every day, week, month, and year with cash you earned, or otherwise acquired, and didn't spend. Add to your treasure continuously. Make it a habit.

CHAPTER 8

PUBLIC TRANSIT – PERSONAL INVESTING

The four most dangerous words in investing are
"This time it's different."

– John Templeton

In a July 2008 episode of *Money File*, Chuck Jaffe, senior columnist at *Marketwatch*, described the wisdom of Sir John Templeton:

> *Years ago, Sir John Templeton identified the four most danger-*
> *ous words in investing as "this time, it's different." Well, for the*
> *investment world in the current, distressed market, this time it*
> *is different, because for the first time since the Great Depression,*
> *Templeton is not around to act as a reminder of the resiliency of*

markets. The legendary investor died last week at age 95, with the market appearing poised to reach the condition he was most famous for identifying—the point of maximum pessimism. Templeton described maximum pessimism as the point where there were no buyers left—except for him, of course. As an arch-contrarian, it was precisely the time he found things most attractive, the time to keep your head above market sentiment, the time when you someday look back and go, "that stretch, right there, that is where I made my money." Now, don't forget that Templeton began his investing career in the 1930s, when the Great Depression was still dampening market enthusiasm. In 1939, he famously bought $100 worth of every stock selling for a buck or less on the New York Stock Exchange, and in time, he made a killing. What's clear from everyone who knew the man is that he would have loved the current market environment. He would have preached international diversification, reminded people to go against the herd, and suggested that it's time to be calm and focused, and to leave the pessimism for others. And unless this time it really is different, it's likely that the market will prove him right, again, in time.

The late John Templeton was a legendary investor. Investing made him a billionaire. During his illustrious career, he founded the Templeton Group of mutual funds (now Franklin-Templeton Funds). The quote above references Templeton's conviction that the nature of things —in this case, common stocks and the stock market—dictates their behavior. If you understand the nature of something, you know what to expect. Security prices and securities markets will rise and fall daily, but markets will always rise in value over time. It's inevitable; it's the nature of securities and the securities markets. Currently, the Dow Jones Industrial Average is trading around 10,000, down from a high just above 14,000 in 2007 but up from last year's low near 6,600. The stock market meltdown that started in late 2007 can easily turn a believer into an unbeliever. There are those who fear the market will never come back, but it will. Templeton was right in 1938, and he'll be proven right in this market too. When the market comes back, it'll make many investors millionaires. Give this route serious consideration because it's open to all.

This route, which I call Public Transit, will transport large numbers of people in our busy, crowded society to the Millionaire's Club. Investors can travel on sleek underground cars and high-speed trains that'll transport them to the capital markets of the world and the always exciting and potentially rewarding world of personal investing.

Democratization, a wonderful word, describes a powerful idea. Democratization is a process that empowers large numbers of people, not only politically, but in a number of other aspects of their lives. It describes something moving away from the exclusive control and use of a few and becoming available to the masses. Once upon a time, kings made all the rules people had to abide by. In a modern democracy, the rules are made by representatives of the people for the people. Modern democracy isn't perfect, but it's a considerable improvement over kings.

The computer has ushered in the information age. Computing and the Internet are democratizing information. The wisdom of the ages and the knowledge that formerly was available only to the elite now is becoming more available to anyone with a computer. More than ever, the average person has access to much of the same information that formerly was available to only a few. This phenomenon is affecting society in many profound ways.

One area where the information age is empowering individuals is investing, which is an activity that has produced many millionaires. Some, like Warren Buffett, the Oracle of Omaha, are famous. Several decades ago, Buffett started with a few thousand dollars and turned it into billions. Buffett is still at it and better than ever. He'll soon be eighty and has no plans to retire. Peter Lynch, George Soros, William O'Neil, T. Rowe Price, the late John Templeton, and scores of others took this road to prosperity. Because information is becoming democratized, including investment-related information, anyone who's willing to spend the time needed to learn about investing can travel this road to personal prosperity.

The first mutual fund—the Massachusetts Investment Trust, which was created in 1928—represents the first significant democratization of personal investing. Mutual funds, which are a fantastic success story, have enabled thousands of people to accumulate personal wealth by investing in securities. In a mutual fund, small investors pool modest amounts of money and allow a professional money manager to invest the money for them. Today personal computing and the Internet are among the tools that empower individual investors, who can do their own research on the Internet and buy and sell securities directly online.

Almost anyone can learn to be an investor. I'm not talking about someone who wants to gamble and play the market; I'm referring to someone who's willing to get an education in finance at a university or by self-study. If you jump in and start investing without some knowledge, you're likely to lose money.

ABOUT INVESTING

There are hundreds of books, articles, newspaper columns, magazines, Web sites, and radio and TV shows, as well as college-level courses and adult continuing-education classes, devoted to investment advice and information. Investment information is in the public domain for those who look for it. A well-stocked public library has almost everything you need to know about investing; however, one significant problem is the volume of information available. There's too much, and it can be overwhelming. Furthermore, the information isn't consistent. There are varying views and opinions and dozens of approaches to investing. People who are deemed to be experts disagree about many things. There are many investment gurus too. Some believe they've discovered the Rosetta Stone of investing and will share their secret with you for a fee. Many investment gurus don't stand the test of time.

A new investor can get started on the wrong foot and make many mistakes. Too many mistakes, or one big one, can derail your journey and wreck your chances for success. Great care is needed. You need to spend time preparing. But because personal investing offers such great opportunity for financial success, it's worth the effort.

This book is not the place to undertake the Herculean task of covering the entire spectrum of investing. I'll limit the discussion to two popular and proven methods used to make money in common stocks—fundamental and technical analysis.

Much of this chapter represents the approach taken by Warren Buffett and William O'Neil. I'll mention several other successful investors such as Peter Lynch, the legendary manager of the Fidelity Magellan Mutual Fund in the late '80s and early

'90s, and Christopher Brown, a value investor who uses an approach similar to Buffett's.

Buffett is the chairman and CEO of a publicly traded company, Berkshire Hathaway. His success as an investor is widely known, and on any given day, either he or Bill Gates is the richest man in the world. Buffett is a value investor, which means he favors buying the stock of what he considers to be a successful company or great business at a fair price or discount.

O'Neil is the founder and CEO of the William J. O'Neil Company and the investment newspaper, *Investor's Business Daily* (IBD). He's a growth investor and advocates buying the stocks of growing companies. He'll buy at a high price (not a discount) and expects the price to climb even higher because the products and services of the company are in demand and sales and earnings are growing dramatically.

To become an investor, you need to have money to invest. Perhaps it's in the form of accumulated savings, a bonus, an inheritance, or an income tax refund. Many people set aside a portion of their income regularly for investment purposes. Many millionaires simply took modest sums of money they acquired from time to time and invested it. Almost anyone can do the same.

Before we discuss fundamental and technical analysis and value and growth investing let's first consider if you want to work with a financial adviser or be a do-it-yourself investor. Historically, lots of investors worked with a financial adviser to make investment decisions. There's plenty of help available for those people who want professional help with investing. Most people don't have the knowledge, time, or inclination to do it on their own. Almost every financial institution you deal with offers some level of assistance making investment decisions. Licensed stockbrokers, investment advisers, and financial planners are trained to help you. Historically, investors who worked with a financial adviser earned better returns on their investments than investors who made their own investment decisions, according to DALBAR, a Boston-based investment research organization. Many investors use the services of professionals and are satisfied with the results. Good financial advice is priceless. If you choose to work with a financial adviser, the only work you need to do is find the right institutions and advisers. You have to pay these organizations and individuals for their services, but success is worth it.

For those who think working with an adviser makes the most sense, find an adviser with whom you can develop a successful relationship. To have a successful relationship, you need to learn enough about investing so you have the right expectations about the results the adviser is achieving.

Trusting your financial adviser isn't enough for success. Thousands of investors trust their financial advisers, and thousands of trustworthy financial advisers work in the best interests of their clients; but financial institutions are in the business of making a profit, and financial advisers are in it to make a living. In some cases, these interests compete with one another, and the investor gets hurt. Don't be naive. People tend to act in their own self-interests, even financial advisers. Remember Bernard Madoff? He took working in his own best interest to a new level. He admittedly deceived his clients in a Ponzi scheme and stole billions from them, ruining thousands of people's lives.

Even when you use professionals, you should know something about investments and investing. Too many investors have an unrealistic sense of what to expect. In these cases, the investor becomes disillusioned about investing and disappointed with the adviser when expectations aren't met. If you have a good sense of what results to expect, you're more likely to have a productive relationship with an adviser and more success investing. You'll have a better sense of when an adviser is performing well. Here's what to expect.

Financial instruments, such as stocks and bonds, fluctuate in price throughout the day. Price fluctuations can occur on a moment's notice. Over several months, prices can trend upward then downward. In other cases, even over the course of a day, price changes can be radical, spiking upward quickly and moving down in a freefall or remaining unchanged for an extended time. There are periods, such as the one we're in, called contractions, in which prices fall dramatically and can stay down for months or a few years. Then there are periods of expansion where prices climb and stay high for an extended period, such as the expansion we experienced during the 1990s. But it's difficult to remember the happy days of the '90s when anyone could make money in the market. The economy is on its ear, and the stock market has lost billions of dollars of value. It's difficult to believe anyone could make a fortune as an investor, but the famous aforementioned investors are still rich, even in this miserable economic climate.

Market movements can't be predicted accurately or consistently. Occasionally, someone will try to demonstrate he or she devised a method of predicting these movements. Such people receive attention and notoriety for a time, but ultimately, the market fools them and everyone who's adopted their method. Future market results are unknown, and this is part of what you should expect. If the value of your investment has declined and hasn't recovered for several years, it doesn't necessarily indicate your financial adviser is inept. If you're down, and the market is up, that's another story.

If you look at published information from credible sources such as Ibbotson Associates (now a part of Morningstar, a Chicago-based investment research organization), you'll see, over time, stocks outperform bonds and real estate, and bonds outperform cash in terms of return. Small company stocks outperform large company stocks. Thus, stocks, in general, are a reasonable security in which to make money over time. This isn't true for every time period, but it's true throughout most extended periods, generally ten to fifteen years or more. History indicates you reasonably can expect to make more money by investing in stocks than other securities if your investment goals are long-term growth of your investment. Remember, there are few hard-and-fast universal rules or truths when it comes to investing, but there are always exceptions. That's why you need to acquire knowledge about investing. Investment success is a moving target.

Historically, the stock market has averaged between 8 to 12 percent a year. Corporate bonds have averaged between 5 to 8 percent. Since the Great Depression in the 1930s, annual returns on stocks as a group, in a given year, have approached 150 percent in the U.S. domestic markets, and logged in losses exceeding 50 percent in down years. There are spectacular years and terribly disappointing years, but the average is 8 to 12 percent. Depending on the date you start and end your calculation and which stock category you're averaging, you'll come up with an average between 8 and 12 percent. Using the past as a guide, that's what you should expect of a broadly diversified portfolio, such as a mutual fund.

That's not to say higher returns aren't possible. They are. One of the ways higher returns might be generated is to find mutual fund managers who can beat the market averages. That's what made Peter Lynch famous. Another approach to beating the averages is to reduce the number of securities you invest in to a smaller group of carefully selected stocks and/or put your money into the hands of an exceptionally good stock picker (fund manager) who does the same thing. One stock can make you rich. Buffett owns stock in Berkshire Hathaway, and the average annualized return on that one stock is more than 20 percent. Berkshire Hathaway owns the stock of many other companies, such as Coke, Proctor & Gamble, and GEICO Insurance. Many people can point to one stock, such as Berkshire Hathaway, IBM, Proctor & Gamble, Microsoft, Google, or Wal-Mart, as the one investment responsible for their million-dollar net worth. Forrest Gump, the fictional protagonist in the book and movie of the same name, made millions with Apple Computer stock thanks to the insight of his friend and business partner, Lieutenant Dan. Hundreds of real people became rich with Apple too. Many portfolios benefit disproportionately from one or a few stocks that produce exceptional returns. But investing in one bad stock can result in losing most, if not all, of your money. Think Enron, WorldCom, or AIG. You never bet on one company alone. If you do, it isn't investing, it's speculation.

While average returns may be sufficient for many investors to achieve their goals, some determine the average returns of the market aren't adequate for their purposes. Some may not want to wait twenty to forty years to access the Millionaire's Club. In these cases, higher-than-average returns are required. Investing for higher returns comes with more risk. But careful securities selection has delivered the desired returns in the past. There's no reason to believe it won't be the same in the future. Templeton believed in the resiliency of the financial markets, and it made him rich. Many investors are looking for what Lynch calls a forty bagger, which is when an original investment increases forty times. So $1,000 invested turns into $40,000. A one hundred bagger is more exciting. The idea is to earn this increase during a short period, a few years. It has been done in the past, and it'll happen in the future too.

The fundamental issue in investing centers on risk and return. If you take more risk, you may earn higher returns. If you take less risk, you must accept lower returns than are otherwise possible. Those who have more time available to accumulate wealth and more money to commit to investments can accumulate enough money to accomplish their financial goals with limited risk. Those who have less time and money, or those who want to maximize their returns, may take the higher risks as a condition of trying to earn high returns quicker. Assuming an investor understands the risks associated with investing for higher returns and knows how to manage them, he or she can succeed.

Risk, in the mind of the novice investor, is the possibility of losing all his or her money. Although many people have managed to lose all their money, a knowledgeable investor wouldn't invest in something where his or her investment is at risk of total loss. Such a commitment of money would be speculation or gambling. But even the best investors make mistakes and buy a security that loses value. That's why an investor never invests exclusively in one stock or security. Diversification is one way an investor manages risk. A wise investor always diversifies by holding numerous securities.

Securities markets behave in a random, unpredictable manner. We haven't learned how to predict the market or control it. Throughout the best part of the past century, we have learned to deal with it. Investors, such as Templeton, believe market values will increase over time just like prices of almost anything. Investors believe certain types of securities, such as stocks, will appreciate more than others. What we don't know is the timing of these things. We also don't know which sectors of the market or which of the thousands of securities will do best in any given time frame. In the future, the securities markets are expected to behave much the same way as they have in the past, but the individual stocks and sectors that perform best are almost certain to be different from the past. As Mark Twain said, "History does not repeat itself, but it does rhyme." The future will be similar to the past, but it won't be exactly the same. The same is true of the securities markets.

Even an investor who works with a financial adviser needs to make sure he or she has a fundamental knowledge of securities investing and knows how the financial markets behave; otherwise, this road will look too treacherous to travel. At the first big market meltdown, the ignorant investor will panic and instruct his or her financial adviser to sell, which, in turn, will result in a substantial investment loss. Then he or she will vow never to invest again. I've always been amazed at the number of people who expect their advisers to make money every day, all the time. No one, other than Bernie Madoff, has ever done that.

Before we discuss a do-it-yourself approach to investing, let's look at preserving your investment gains. Some investors take a buy-and-hold approach to investing. The idea is they'll never, or rarely, sell anything they've purchased. They'll ride out the ups and downs of the market knowing it behaves this way and, ultimately, will make money because they purchased the stock of well-performing businesses.

Some investors use a sell discipline rather than hold securities through the ups and downs of the market. Their view is that substantial declines of the value of investments are unacceptable. If you own a stock worth $100, and it decreases to $50, the investment has lost 50 percent of its value, and it'll take a 100 percent increase of the value of a $50 stock to get back to $100. The comeback can take a long time; therefore, some investors sell once they experience a decline in value of 8 percent to 10 percent. The problem is that daily market fluctuations can easily exceed 8 to 10 percent. The cost of buying and selling and the tax consequences, not to mention the record keeping, makes this a complex approach; but it's the cost of preserving your gains.

Another approach is hedging. For instance, hedge funds use sophisticated strategies designed to preserve capital. Holding stocks and gold in your portfolio would represent a simple hedging strategy. Gold's value tends to increase during gloomy economic periods when stocks decline. These two tend to offset one another and limit your losses. More sophisticated approaches to hedging involve using options, futures and short selling. A seasoned investor may resort to the use of such measures to preserve gains. Read O'Neil's book, *How to Make Money in Stocks,* to learn more about a sell discipline.

If you're going to go it alone and become a do-it-yourself investor, some quick-start educational tools include O'Neil's book, Christopher Brown's *The Little Book of Value Investing*, and Lynch's books *One Up on Wall Street*, *Beat the Street,* and *Learn to Earn.* Lynch outperformed the benchmark S&P 500 stock index each consecutive year he ran the fund, which was a feat never accomplished by any fund manager to that point. You may also want to read publications such as *Barron's* and *Investor's Business Daily* and subscribe to services such as the Value Line Investment Survey, Standard & Poor's, or Morningstar. These are excellent investor resources, which are available at the public library.

You also may want to consider a membership in one of the associations serving the needs of individual investors. An organization such as the American Association of Individual Investors will help you get an investment education. These aren't the only credible resources available to novice investors, but they're a good start.

You'll also find resources and educational materials at the websites for on-line brokers such as Scottrade, TD Ameritrade, and Charles Schwab and Company. Insightful magazines, such as *Kiplinger's Personal Finance* and *Forbes* also are valuable resources.

You shouldn't become an investor by jumping in and trading. Many novice investors attend a road show that comes to their city with the promise of giving them the secrets needed to succeed as an investor. In some cases, the initial seminar is free, but it ends with an opportunity to buy something. It might be a trading platform, a book or other media package, coaching or classes at a forum or retreat. It'll cost you if you buy into these programs. Some cost thousands. These are compelling presentations that include testimonials given by people who've succeeded with the product or program presented. These propositions teach you how to invest on your own online. If you're interested, you need to make sure you're not paying for something that might cost a lot less, or perhaps even be free, from another source. Some of the stock, options, and commodities exchanges put on free road shows to promote trading in the particular item traded on their exchange. Get an investment education. Be careful, do your homework, and don't be naïve.

The thrifty people we discussed in the last chapter should consider investing some of their savings in the stock market. Most people need to earn returns higher than bank deposits and bonds because they have limited resources and time to accomplish their goals. Investing in securities and real estate offers the potential to earn the higher returns needed to supercharge some or most of your savings. Investments with double-digit returns represent a means for large numbers of people to accumulate a million dollars or more in less than a working career.

Here are the six basic rules that apply to investing:

1. Diversification – Never put all your eggs in one basket. Own anywhere from ten to several dozen individual securities. Investing in a mutual fund or exchange traded fund (ETF) provides diversification.

2. Invest in individual securities or funds that have a realistic possibility to increase in value over time. Cash doesn't appreciate in value. Because of inflation, cash loses value over time. So unless you're a currency trader, consider something else. The value of common stocks and real estate fluctuates, but the long-term trend is upward. Although appreciation on real estate is similar to the return on bonds, many real estate purchases are made in conjunction with leverage or borrowing. Buying a $100,000 property with $20,000 or less down, where rent pays the mortgage, increases the return on real estate. Because we're in the midst of a real estate catastrophe, many people have lost their shirts, and the mess is so bad, many will never recover their losses. But it's an ideal time

to buy real estate. Unfortunately, those who purchased real estate with borrowed money during the boom that preceded the recent bust are in big trouble if they have to sell their property. Those who can buy real estate now with cash or borrowed money can make a killing. An old axiom in real estate is you make money on real estate when you buy it, not when you sell it. It's currently a buyer's market for real estate and stocks.

3. Reinvest your earnings. If a stock pays a dividend, reinvest it and buy more. When an investor or mutual fund sells securities and a profit is made, reinvest it. Reinvest excess rent in more real estate. This compounding makes a significant contribution to the growth of your investment over time. It can represent as much as half of the increase in the value of an investment.

4. Minimize your costs. Every dollar you pay in fees and trading costs is a dollar not available to invest. The average fee charged by a mutual fund is more than 2 percent per year, and that doesn't include any commissions paid to the representative who may have sold the fund to an investor. Commissions and fees vary widely, and unless you're getting a superior result, you should be looking for low fees and commissions. If you're trading securities, the commissions per trade reduce your return, as well. You need to use approaches to investing designed to keep your costs down. Buying securities and holding them (not trading) is a common, low-cost approach to investing.

5. Minimize taxes on your investment activities. Taxes are another cost, which Congress raises and lowers over time to accommodate the political and economic agenda at the time. As a general rule, you want to avoid paying taxes on investments, and where taxes are paid, you want to pay only a capital gains tax, which suggests buying and holding individual securities or investing in mutual funds that attempt to minimize taxes. Trading is expensive because it costs money each time you buy and sell and because short-term gains result in the payment of ordinary income tax (which is higher than capital gains taxes) if you make a profit. Trading isn't for rookies or the average investor.

6. Take advantage of time. The longer you stay invested, the more likely it is that you will not only preserve your principal, but you'll receive acceptable returns.

In terms of personal investing as a route to millions, there are many trains that lead to riches. There are many approaches, methods, and strategies an investor can choose. Some will take you there faster than others, but the risks are much higher than on a slower train. A derailment can end your quest for wealth. Purchasing mutual funds such as Vanguard's Index 500 Fund, or exchange-traded funds like SPIDERS, a security that replicates the S&P 500 stock market index or QQQQ (an index security that closely replicates the performance of the largest one hundred stocks that trade on the NASDAQ) makes sense for the novice investor. Partly because there are no fund managers, these funds have low expenses and there are seldom any trading expenses. Holding these funds for long periods is a sensible approach to becoming a successful investor.

On the other hand, many noteworthy actively managed mutual funds charge higher fees but perform well. Lynch managed such a fund at Fidelity Investments and made an above-average return and a lot of money for many happy people.

American Funds has an excellent reputation and track record, along with T. Rowe Price and Legg Mason. There are thousands of actively managed mutual funds, but only a handful consistently beat the market. Thus, investing in index funds is popular because most fund managers don't do as well as the indexes and costs are lower. But there's evidence that certain types of investing are best handled by an active manager. Investing in the stocks of smaller companies, investing internationally and investing in companies in emerging world markets, such as Asia, or new industries, such as biotech, usually requires the know-how and insights of active managers. You can't ignore active management, especially if these managers are delivering results. In these cases, the fees and expenses are justified.

You may hear a lot of talk about doing your own trading online. There are countless advertisements encouraging would-be investors to jump into the investment fray in this way. Professional traders make money despite the costs and taxes. A new investor doesn't have the benefit of their knowledge and experience.

Many high-profile investors, such as Buffett, tend to buy and hold. They're interested in acquiring a stake in what they consider to be a successful business that makes great profits and generates and accumulates lots of cash. They never intend to sell these securities. Lynch, on the other hand, sold securities once they no longer possessed the characteristics that prompted him to buy them in the first place. O'Neil and Brown elaborate on a sell discipline in their books as well. You have to learn what, how, and when to buy, but you also have to know when and how you are going to sell, if you're going to sell at all.

All of these investment legends use fundamental analysis when evaluating stocks—they *investigate the company behind the stock* and look for a solid, successful company in which they want to take an ownership position. Fundamental analysis involves evaluating many things including the current price of the stock, sales of the company, profitability, debt, how much stock managers of the business own, return on assets, past, present and future earnings, and other factors that are indicative of the health of a business, the success of the company, and its future prospects.

Technical analysis is another popular approach to investing in which the investor *tracks the behavior of a security* in the market, using charts and formulas that indicate the trend of the stocks price and signal when to buy and sell. Charting securities behavior has become much easier with the personal computer and Internet. When you look at a computer screen and can pull up charts and graphs, you're viewing the tools of the technician or chartist. Fundamental and technical analysis are used widely. Some investors, such as O'Neil, embrace aspects of both. But learning what fundamental analysis is and how to use it is the first step in acquiring the skills of a master investor. In fundamental analysis, an investor also looks at cash flow, dividends, management experience and expertise, market dominance of the company, and a variety of factors that contribute to making the business successful and that fuel the growth of value over time. The superstar investors who have risen to legendary status all embraced this fundamental approach. Acquiring a solid understanding of technical analysis and how to apply it comes next.

There are traders who make money on Wall Street and Main Street every day. Even novice investors have made money and succeeded in the trading game. A good day trader can make a thousand dollars a day or more. If you're a novice investor, the bottom line is, be cautious. Too many people jump into the game with a little money as if they're playing a video game. Many lose their shirts.

As noted earlier, large numbers of people have an opportunity to participate in an employer-sponsored 401(k) profit-sharing plan or similar arrangement. The chance to participate in such a plan represents a significant opportunity to accumulate wealth during a working career. Having contributions from your wages deposited into such a tax-exempt trust—often enhanced by employer contributions, and then invested in diversified mutual funds—represents an excellent means of accumulating wealth. These plans, by themselves, will transport thousands of people to the Millionaire's Club. If such an arrangement is available, take advantage of it.

Those who invest in a 401(k) plan may not have the help of a financial adviser. With such a plan, you're responsible for making your own investment decisions. You decide which of the available mutual fund options are appropriate for you. Some know-how is required; otherwise, the opportunity can be wasted. But if you have a financial adviser, perhaps he or she can assist you in making 401(k) investment decisions too. In other cases, your employer may provide educational assistance or investment advisory help. Take advantage of anything that may be available.

Investments in real estate make a lot of sense for many investors. There are a plethora of books, seminars, road shows, and all-night cable TV infomercials espousing the merits of real estate investing. Generally speaking, the techniques and strategies presented are legitimate. Real estate has made millionaires of many people. An investor could invest in real estate directly or in the form of a security such as a real estate investment trust (REIT). Much of the information about successful real estate investing is devoted to direct investment in real property. Direct investment offers the possibility of greater returns but requires much more work, time, and attention than owning a REIT that invests in real estate. When you hold a direct investment in real estate, it requires attention. The phone rings all the time, and there's always an issue or problem to address. Those who do their homework and take the time to educate themselves may find real estate is their ticket to financial success.

In terms of commodities such as gold, silver, pork bellies, and gasoline, the risk is so high, and the level of sophistication so great, commodities investing is only for those who are educated and prepared to consider these instruments. Likewise, investments in specialty items, such as collectibles, are beyond the scope of this discussion. The big fortunes that have been discussed here were amassed by investing in stocks.

UPSIDE

This road is open to everyone. You can become a millionaire, multimillionaire, or perhaps even a billionaire. Financial security can be yours, and you can enjoy the freedom only financial independence can offer. You can choose a slower more predictable train, or you can board a high-speed coach; the destination is the same in either case. It's not a high-risk ride to the Millionaire's Club for the educated investor.

DOWNSIDE

You have to prepare yourself—read or attend courses about investing. Do both. You need to embrace a discipline and be a patient investor to succeed. You also need to practice, go slow, and learn from the inevitable mistakes you'll make. Some recommend novice investors buy and sell on paper before they commit money. There are Web sites that accommodate this type of virtual investing. It takes time. If you're foolish, the market will take your money. This is a thinking person's game. There's no place for emotion in sound investing. Fear and greed have brought countless investors to ruin. In the end, there's some guesswork in investing. An investor is making well-informed and educated guesses. Even the most successful investors make mistakes. Those who succeed guess right enough times to make a fortune.

IS PERSONAL INVESTING YOUR ROAD TO RICHES?

In the information age, more people will take on the task of personal investing. With the information and tools at your fingertips, those of you who want to do it yourself will be empowered to do so. But the six aforementioned rules still apply to you. Successful investors are people like you and me. Some are well educated, and others have had the benefit of learning their craft from the masters. Many are intelligent and insightful, but many are average people who were willing to study and carefully apply what they learned.

Some aspects of investing are complex and demanding, but a simple strategy of buying and holding a diversified fund of securities over a long period of time works too. That may be all that's required. I've met, talked with, and worked for a number of people who took this simple approach to investing and earned a membership in the Millionaire's Club.

You're free to learn about investing and acquire the required skills and apply them. No one is going to stop you. Personal investing is one road to riches large numbers of us can travel successfully.

HOW TO SUCCEED AS AN INVESTOR:

- Learn about investing. Read books, and take classes or a course about the subject. Become literate in business, finance, and investing.
- Decide if you want to be a do-it-yourself investor or if you want to work with an adviser. If you work with an adviser, try to participate rather than simply follow his or her recommendations. Understand the why of the recommendations and learn from the experience.
- If you go it alone, be conservative first. Practice on a virtual Web site. Become a student of investing and acquire a reasonable knowledge about the subject.
- Start slow. Invest in mutual funds and exchange traded funds and do so in a 401(k) plan or a personal IRA if possible. Select indexed funds with low fees and trading costs or target dated funds. Then you can move some of your investment dollars into individual stocks and real estate.
- Invest reasonable sums of money. The more you invest, the more you can make. Hopefully, you can set aside 10 percent of wages or more each year for investments.

- Favor stocks because they offer the highest return potential. You have to manage risk through diversification, too. There's a place for bonds, real estate, and cash in your strategy, particularly as you grow older.
- Expect the market to go up and down and spike and crash from time to time.
- Always diversify; never put all of your eggs in one basket.
- Purchase investments that have the potential to appreciate over time.
- Reinvest your earnings.
- Keep your cost low.
- Minimize taxes on your investment activities.
- Be a long-term investor.

CHAPTER 9

FORMER MILLIONAIRES / STARTING OVER, STARTING LATE

A fool and his money are soon parted.
— **Thomas Tusser**

You absolutely, positively don't want to become a former millionaire! Once you have a seven-figure net worth, you need to keep it. Having made the journey, paid your dues, relished the pride and satisfaction of accomplishment, and achieved your goal, you don't want to go back. Life is better with money than without it. Losing your wealth is awful.

So, you need to reduce risk once wealth has been acquired. Once you have it, you need to build a fortress around it, manage it with care, and insulate it from loss.

Some would argue keeping wealth is more difficult than acquiring it. Perhaps it is equally difficult. But, in any case, the old adage, "A fool and his money are soon parted," is still true. Not everyone who has lost his or her fortune is a fool, but many have lost it because they were foolish. For others, ignorance results in the loss of wealth.

Recently, a woman in the Cleveland area won a huge lottery jackpot. She was a working woman with a regular job, and her husband ran a small mom-and-pop business. Now she's a multimillionaire. But she refused to be interviewed by journalists and, other than a brief public statement, she dropped out of sight. However, she was sighted walking into the offices of Ernst & Young, the international accounting and consulting firm. I have no idea how much this woman knows about money, but she apparently wasn't taking any chances. She sought out the smartest people she could think of to give her advice. I have no idea if she had an education from a prestigious university or if she graduated from the school of hard knocks, but she exhibited remarkable common sense. This is a pretty savvy woman, and I'll bet she doesn't become a former millionaire.

In my work as a financial planner, I've talked with, interviewed, and worked for hundreds of successful people who made a lot of money. Most were millionaires and managed to hang on to their wealth, but some didn't.

Sometimes a once-successful business collapses, and the owner is faced with bankruptcy. Competitors can move in on your business and finish you off in no time, and technology and innovation can render your business obsolete. So those who have all their wealth tied up in a business face many challenges that threaten their survival, thinking their business is invincible, which is foolish.

Greed and fear have caused the loss of many investment fortunes. For some, the more they have, the more they want, so they take unnecessary risks. When it comes to investments, cool heads need to prevail. Emotional and psychological interference with rational thinking can cause an investor to lose millions.

I recall an interview I once read about a successful and prolific entrepreneur. This man started and developed half a dozen successful businesses. Once he established a business and it was operating well, he sold it. The journalist asked why he sold all of these great businesses, and he replied business is a dangerous proposition and may not last long term. For him, it was better to develop a business idea into a successful operation, then sell it at a profit and invest those proceeds in assets of enduring value. The journalist asked, "What are assets of enduring value?" The entrepreneur glibly replied that stocks, bonds, and real estate represented such assets.

There's wisdom here. This guy was a successful entrepreneur and probably knew creating a new business was his strength and talent. So he kept doing the entrepreneurial thing over and over again. Maybe he wasn't a successful operator. He may not have had sound management and financial skills, and perhaps he would've ruined these businesses if he tried to run them long term. He also had a keen appreciation for the vulnerabilities of a business. There are businesses that have survived the test of time, but the nature of business is such that most die off over relatively short time periods. Most don't survive beyond one generation of ownership.

Historically, among those businesses that survive for one generation, only one-third survive for a second generation and only 10 to 15 percent last for three generations. A Small Business Administration study recently updated these numbers. They're worse. The study stated only 5 percent of new businesses survive beyond a third generation—mortality among businesses is high. Many of the survivors are the General Electrics and Proctor & Gambles of the world. Successful survivors are well managed, but ultimately, new technology, competition, or both can do in a well-established business. Think General Motors.

Given this mortality, a small business isn't an asset of enduring value. So our savvy entrepreneur takes his money and invests it in stocks, bonds, and real estate.

If you look at where rich people have their wealth, it's in stocks, bonds, and real estate. They own business assets too, because successful businesses produce more wealth. They diversify into other asset classes to reduce risk and remain wealthy. As we can see today, even though some stocks have lost value, the market is recovering and most quality stocks have seen their value restored. Likewise, although some bonds go into default, most do well over time. Some real estate assets turn out to be worthless, while others hold their value and appreciate. There are still plenty of high-quality investments in which you can store wealth. The companies owned by Berkshire Hathaway, operated by Warren Buffett, are good examples.

I once gave a speech in which I talked about former millionaires and assets of enduring value. After the talk, a retired partner from a large international accounting firm stopped to talk with me. He cheerfully agreed with everything I had to say about the subject. His wealth was entirely invested in a diversified portfolio of insured municipal bonds. These bonds weren't only issued by a government entity that taxes its constituents to make good on the interest and principal payments, but they were insured by a third-party insurance company against default in any case. It was real insurance, not credit default swaps such as those used at AIG.

Assets of enduring value are affected by market cycles and economic events, but such cycles and events don't turn all such assets into worthless property. Eventually, values return and exceed pre-catastrophe levels. If you became a member of the Millionaire's Club just before the big decline, you may have lost your membership because the value of your assets declined to something below one million dollars. However, had you reduced the risk of such a substantial decline, by taking positions in assets that are less volatile, you very well may have preserved your membership and financial security.

There are numerous considerations for those who've acquired wealth and intend to preserve it. They include insurance and asset protection strategies. In this book, we're primarily concerned with entering the Millionaire's Club. We won't spend a lot of time here talking about wealth preservation. But once you have it, you don't want to lose it. You need to have a plan to keep your wealth. Don't leave your good fortune to chance. Once some people become wealthy, they become a little cocky and feel invincible, which is dangerous. A little humility may help you preserve your wealth.

A number of professionals and financial institutions work with the affluent to enhance and preserve their wealth. Once you have the assets, you'll receive a lot of attention from these folks, but take great care when selecting advisers. You need them when you're wealthy. Yet many wealthy people have been duped by con men in $1,000 suits over $500 lunches. Be careful.

People who have successful executive jobs often receive financial planning services and advice as a perk or benefit. Generally speaking, this is high-quality advice. Much of it comes from accounting firms, consulting organizations, law firms and financial institutions. There's plenty of sound advice available. Like the lottery winner mentioned earlier, you need to seek out good advice. When you get it, follow it. I've known wealthy people who receive great advice, pay top dollar for it and don't follow it. Many end up losing their fortune as a consequence. Wealthy people who stay wealthy also make it their business to learn about wealth and how it's managed and preserved. Even though they use advisers, they make it their business to understand the fundamentals of wealth preservation. Hopefully, the wealthy ancestors of heirs and heiresses have taken steps to preserve and enhance family wealth in perpetuity. In so doing, the financial independence of heirs and heiresses is assured. Professional athletes, superstar entertainers, as well as some celebrities, have agents who work hard to preserve the wealth of their clients. Large-income professionals and many of those with high-level executive jobs receive professional financial advice as an executive benefit.

For the rest of us—those working regular jobs with the right employer, those practicing thrift or succeeding in sales—we need help too. If financial advice isn't available to you, develop a relationship with a financial planner. Don't be overly self-confident about keeping the wealth you've acquired. Keeping it requires a different skill set than the one you needed to acquire it. Again, take responsibility for preserving your wealth but get professional help too. If you are educated and well informed in matters of personal finance, you'll make better decisions regarding the advice your financial adviser gives you. Be smart and maintain your membership in the Millionaire's Club.

STARTING OVER/STARTING LATE

Satchel Page was one of the greatest baseball pitchers to ever take the field. Because he was black, and blacks weren't permitted to play in Major League Baseball before 1947, Page spent his prime in the obscurity of Negro League Baseball. When he was in his forties, he followed Jackie Robinson into the majors. He stunned and pleased baseball fans in Cleveland (the Indians gave him his first contract) and throughout the country with his spectacular pitching. When asked about how he felt about being left out of the majors for so long he said, *Don't look back. Something might be gaining on you.* He didn't look back. He took advantage of his current good fortune. He focused on the moment and did the best he could with the present opportunity.

Many people get a late start when it comes to financial success. There are any number of reasons. Some suffer setbacks, perhaps catastrophic. Some have the best intentions early in life, but things go wrong. Maybe you started strong in your financial life but were distracted or something slowed you down. Perhaps you didn't do a good job of catching up. Maybe you became a millionaire but, unbelievably, lost it. Maybe you're retired and are neither a millionaire nor the equivalent millionaire. You might be in your fifties without any money set aside for the future.

Is it too late for you if you don't have another thirty or forty years to accumulate wealth? Can you afford to take risks at your age? Is your fate sealed? Is it ever too late to get started? Can you experience a financial catastrophe, such as a divorce, bankruptcy, death of a breadwinner, or serious illness or disability, and make a comeback?

It's difficult to make up for lost time, and your options may be limited. You may have to accept more risk as a condition of trying to catch up. Many people have had to start over in life, sometimes more than once, and many have succeeded. It's certainly possible to start late or start over and succeed.

Your attitude and level of energy and enthusiasm are important considerations. Sometimes people give up and quit. People suffer from burnout, but human beings are amazingly resilient too. We can suffer enormous setbacks yet return to the action. If your attitude is positive, health is reasonably good, and spirit isn't broken, you still can become a millionaire. Where there's a will, there's a way. Remember, this is America.

I read an article about a self-employed professional who was in his fifties. He had a panic attack because the reality of his financial situation was so dire. He had nothing set aside for retirement and spent every penny he earned. Other than the equity in his home, he had no assets. He was in trouble and decided to do something to provide for himself and his wife as they grew older. He looked at a number of things and decided that investing was his best shot for redemption.

Since succeeding was so critical, he decided he couldn't delegate the task to an investment adviser or financial planner. He had to do it himself, so he read all he could find about investing. The process took a couple of years, but he eventually felt confident about his newfound knowledge. He did all the things disciplined investors do while continuing to make a living. In the end, he did something that's never recommended by advisers—he put all his eggs in one basket. He did so because he had limited resources. All he had to invest was the equity in his home, so he bet the farm. He took a long shot and made an educated bet on one company. It was a big risk, and many people would call it a foolish one. He invested in a small company that made a public stock offering several years earlier and seemed positioned for substantial growth. He placed his bet and bought as many shares as he could. He won. He took the equity in his home and turned it into almost $2 million in a few years.

This story reminds me of a famous quote attributed to both Mark Twain and Andrew Carnegie, the late industrialist and multimillionaire: "Put all your eggs in one basket and...watch that basket!"

Why did he succeed? It may have been luck, but most likely, it was his initiative and the quality of his analysis. He focused on a serious problem and solved it. He didn't buy any stock; he bought into a company he investigated carefully and thoroughly. Then he watched that investment closely.

One stock can make you rich, but one stock can make you poor too. This individual took a huge risk, but he became an expert. He didn't take a blind chance; he took an educated, well-informed chance.

This individual traveled one of the twelve routes that lead to prosperity and got there quickly. He started late but, fortunately, he was able to catch up.

Colonel Sanders was sixty-five years old before he tried to sell his fried chicken recipe to restaurant owners, and it took several years for him to succeed. He started late in life because he was broke and wasn't willing to live on the small income he had. He traveled the road of private enterprise—an expressway to wealth—to the Millionaire's Club. You can travel that road at any age.

Successful business owners are always happy to share their story with you. I've heard scores of them firsthand. I recall a sixty-five-year-old business owner who was planning to slow down a bit and let his kids take over the day-to-day operation of his business. He said he was tired, and I assumed he had been hard at work for the past thirty to forty years building the company into the success it had become. But the reason for his tiredness was because he started the company when he was fifty-eight. He said it was difficult to start from scratch and build a company that fast. Really!

I'm aware of a successful business owner whose once-profitable business took a turn for the worse, and he ended up losing the business and had to file personal bankruptcy. He and his family left town in disgrace. He took a job as a salesman and soon found a new opportunity with an emerging company. He became a Wendy's franchisee and not only made a comeback, but surpassed his previous business accomplishments by a large measure. He left town feeling defeated and feeling like a bum only to return a hero. All of this took place after this man was in his fifties. He was back on top and financially independent by the time he was sixty.

The Seiberling brothers started the Goodyear Tire and Rubber Company and became millionaires. The business fell on hard times after World War I, and the company sank into debt. The bankers took over the company and forced the Seiberlings out. They were broke. Within six months, they started the Seiberling Tire Company and made a comeback. The message is don't give up. Successful business ventures can be rocket ships to wealth.

Being frugal may help you cope with the short supply of money and assets late in life, but thrift is no longer a realistic route to consider for wealth accumulation. It's too late to count on saving and frugal living to become a millionaire.

It isn't likely you'll have a shot at professional sports or the entertainment business but some, such as Satchel Page, did. Frank McCourt, who wrote the memoir *Angela's Ashes*, cashed in on the literary talent he possessed later in life.

Landing a high-level executive job isn't likely, but you could become a celebrity. Many people who suffer setbacks in life have a story others are interested to hear. Such a story may inspire others. Some have turned their troubles and tragedies into a business by becoming a speaker or consultant, or by offering a product or service that helps others avoid that pain. Also, getting a job with the right employer could make you financially independent within a relatively short period of time.

Going back to school and earning an undergraduate or graduate degree could give you newfound opportunity. You might even become a professional later in life. People in their fifties do this kind of thing all the time. It isn't easy, but they put themselves in a position where they can win in the end.

Maybe you'll be graced by good luck. I read about an elderly couple who won a lottery jackpot that made them multimillionaires. Age isn't a barrier where luck is concerned.

I've seen many people who were starting over give sales a try. I've seen people come into sales later in life and succeed. I recall the story of a career educator who lost his job and couldn't find another in his field. He was desperate. He finally, and somewhat reluctantly, decided to become an insurance agent. He went on to build a successful and profitable health insurance agency. He made a spectacular come back.

Private enterprise and personal investing are open to anyone at any age. Granted, you may not have much money, but this may be where you have your best shot. A small business based in your home or garage is all you may need to start. Think of the people who've built successful businesses around eBay. There are other legitimate e-commerce opportunities emerging today. A successful blogger could turn his or her journalistic talents into a business. Other people are doing it; you can too.

Opportunities may lie with the seventy-six million aging Baby Boomers. What new businesses will be created to satisfy their needs and desires? What existing businesses will be expanding to serve this group? Is there a business opportunity for you in that population demographic? Succeeding in your own business isn't easy, and good things don't always come quickly. But the road is wide open, and the rewards for those who succeed are substantial.

Personal investing is a risky proposition if you're looking for big returns in the short run. Even if you become an investment phenomenon, it takes money to make money. A huge return on a small amount of money is still only a small amount of money. But assuming you have a reasonable sum to work with, you could become a student of investing and apply what you learn successfully. As I stated earlier, a successful day trader can make $1,000 or more a day.

What is your goal? Your destination is still the Millionaire's Club, and now you're pressed for time. Don't lament your circumstances too long. Don't procrastinate. It's time to get moving!

CHAPTER 10

THE ELEMENTS OF SUCCESS

If you don't know where you are going, any road will take you there.

– Lewis Carroll

To become a millionaire you must successfully travel one of the twelve roads which end at the Millionaire's Club.

The key word is successfully. How do you successfully travel any of these roads? If you want to be a doctor, you have to pass a test to enter medical school. If you fail the test, you can't go to medical school. If you're accepted, you have to graduate. If you do so, you'll have succeeded at entering a profession that can make you rich. If you want to sell, you have to be hired for a sales job and then successfully sell the product or service you signed on to sell. If you do, you're on your way. If you want to work at a regular job on Main Street, you have to do so with the right employer. You have to do homework and identify a great employer. Then you have to be hired. If you're hired, you have to do a good job to remain employed there.

You have to be good at whatever you do to be successful. Investors have to do quality analysis and research to succeed. Entrepreneurs and business owners have to learn how to make a profit and generate and accumulate cash in their businesses; athletes have to perform as expected; and so on. You have to succeed in the endeavors you undertake. How does one succeed?

The prevailing political and economic environments make personal success possible. As far as America is concerned, this critical element is self-completing because the right environment is the democratic and capitalistic system in which we live. Any other similar environment is suitable. America is the land of opportunity. It's an environment that permits and promotes individual success.

Education is another element that contributes to making a person successful, financially or otherwise. Those who have more education, as a group, do better financially than those with less education. This has been well documented. The average person with a college education will earn, on average, more than $1 million more during his or her lifetime than a person without a degree.

Not every person who has a college degree does well financially. On the other hand, there are plenty of examples of people who have little education and became millionaires. Although Bill Gates attended Harvard, he didn't graduate. Gates, and those like him, constitute a minority. Higher education is important for numerous reasons, including its contribution to producing more income and personal wealth. A 2006 *Bloomberg/Los Angeles Times* poll illustrates why education matters. Education is the biggest element separating the affluent from everyone else. Every year of education adds 12 percent more to earnings each year. That's twice as much as a generation ago. A person with a bachelor's degree makes about $32,000 more per year than someone who doesn't graduate from college.

The idea that earning a college education is worthwhile has been disputed recently. Some believe it's not worth it. In fact, there's an increasing number of incidents in which graduates are facing personal bankruptcy because of the expense incurred paying for college. This idea that higher education isn't worth it is misleading and dangerous.

The problem isn't education; it's the cost of education and the financing some students choose as a condition of earning a degree. In situations where parents or grandparents pay college tuition for a student, that student has no debt to pay back after graduation and he or she is getting a great start in life. The student who works his or her way through college and graduates without any debt is off to a great start too. Those students who have an average amount of student loan debt, which is about $20,000, accompanied by a low-interest rate and liberal payback terms, can manage to pay the debt back easily over a reasonable time. In these instances, the cost is worth it.

However, students who have massive amounts of debt, in many cases more than $100,000, are in trouble from the start. Worse yet, many of these high-interest loans are so onerous they may never be paid back. They become a lifetime albatross. These large loans are created often by borrowing to pay every expense associated with attending college. For some students, they continue to borrow to attend graduate and/or professional school. Then they borrow to cover their living expenses while in school, including a social life. Some of these loans aren't low-interest, government-backed loans. Many are supplied by predatory lenders.

Much of this is a consequence of ignorance or, in some cases, a student's stupidity. Colleges and universities need to clean up their act too. They need to do a better job of steering students away from this type of financing. I know people who are still making monthly payments on their student loans while their own children are heading to college. There's something seriously wrong with this.

If we can't get education done right and educate more of the population, our future may not be as successful as our past. Educational opportunities are widely available – that's great – but the cost of education needs to be affordable, and financing an education needs to be available on the most favorable of terms. Parents and students need to keep financing costs to a minimum.

While education on its own can do a lot to improve the chances for more people to become more prosperous, there's more to consider—developing financial skills and forming sound money habits.

According to former Federal Reserve Chairman Alan Greenspan, the country has a problem with financial literacy. Greenspan hit the nail on the head when he described the state of financial literacy in America. According to Greenspan, too many people know too little about money and personal finance, which leads to big mistakes, missed opportunities, and serious errors in judgment. Billionaire investor, Warren Buffett, encourages students to get a financial education as a part of their overall education. Buffett graduated from college, but returned to attend graduate school at Columbia and studied under the acclaimed Benjamin Graham, the father of value investing. Society, as a whole, needs to become more financially literate, one person at a time.

Where do we acquire our financial know-how? Some people may have economic savvy in their genes. Others may get it from their family in their formative years. Culture plays a role, too. To some extent, our education system makes a contribution to our financial knowledge, but too many people don't receive a formal financial education.

Greenspan's sentiments are as much an indictment as they are an observation. There's no formal, comprehensive, official curriculum that addresses financial literacy. We teach our kids how to develop valuable life skills and contribute to society, but we don't teach them enough about their own financial well-being. We teach them how to work and tell them how to get a job, but we don't teach them how to become wealthy and self-reliant.

It isn't as though this situation has gone unnoticed. While there are no formal financial literacy programs, you can find a program in a kindergarten class on the East Coast or at a prestigious university in the Midwest. Some are in the workplace, while consumer advocacy groups, community groups, and financial institutions offer others. Numerous classes, booklets, pamphlets, videos, and Web sites address various financial issues. In most cases, well-qualified, dedicated people put these programs together and administer them. These programs are meant to make a positive improvement in financial literacy, but are they effective?

Look at the mess we're in presently. Consumers spent more than they made and took the equity out of their homes to buy plasma screen televisions, go on vacation, and pay off their high-interest-rate credit cards. In doing so, they took the credit card balance and spread it out over a thirty-year mortgage with an adjustable interest rate. Now that the stock market has collapsed and home values declined substantially, many people are left with few to no assets.

Are we more financially literate today than we were a century ago—a generation ago? Are we doing better financially? Economists say yes because they look at the big picture and the big numbers. Consumer advocates say no. There are disturbing trends.

Real disposable income is declining. The gap between the haves and the have-nots is widening. Even though the total amount of personal wealth is at an all-time high, so is personal debt. No one has done a study on the impact of financial literacy programs, and there's no research to give us an indication if all of this is changing lives for the better. Until recently, there has been no serious effort to institutionalize financial literacy, to make it a part of every person's education. The legislature in Ohio passed a bill into law mandating middle and high school students have financial education included in the math and social studies curriculum. The law took effect in 2008. It's a start.

Rather than limit financial literacy to a few programs, institutions, and students, it should be available more widely. Ideally, financial literacy should be a comprehensive program that's coordinated with, and integrated into, a traditional education from kindergarten through college.

If you sit down with graduating high school seniors— even recent college graduates—and talk to them about money and personal finance, as I have, you'll find they know little about money or how to acquire wealth. According to the Jump$tart Coalition for Financial Literacy, an organization that's chartered to improve financial literacy, high school seniors flunked a financial literacy test for the fifth time in a row, scoring barely more than 50 percent. There was no appreciable improvement in scores since the test was first administered. Professor Lewis Mandell of the University of Buffalo, who conducted the survey and analyzed the tests, said, "The problem is not about to resolve itself any time soon." The test has been administered biannually for the past ten years.

Likewise, financial planners know firsthand few adults have a solid financial foundation. Everyone readily agrees we need better education, better schools, and a more financially savvy population. But no one's willing to do what it takes to change things. For the moment, the cavalry isn't coming. Help isn't on the way—you're on your own. This reality is what makes the role of a financial adviser so important. If you're not as financially literate as you could or should be, it's in your best interest to seek help.

Get as much education as you can. Attend college and graduate at a minimum. College isn't for everyone, but try; and make a financial education a part of your overall education.

We need to improve education in our society if we want America to maintain its stature as a world leader and an economic powerhouse in the future. Someone needs to take financial literacy to the next level and champion the idea of integrating it into the educational curriculum for every student in the country. It should be made available to adults too. An educated, financially savvy population is better equipped to maximize its own resources and take advantage of the opportunities our political and economic systems provide.

There's a serious concern in society about the increasing gap between the rich and the poor. It's an issue with serious implications. The fundamental remedy for the plight of the poor is a better education, a steady job, and more economic opportunity. But in our society, public education is in a freefall, and better jobs require an education. There are economic opportunities for the well educated, but those who have less education are at risk. An education is fundamental to creating a better life for everyone, and an education is available to almost anyone who wants one. The tragedy is about one-third of high school students who enroll in college drop out. There are also an alarming number of students who don't even finish high school, let alone attend college. Although the high school drop out rate has declined over the past two decades it is still 14 percent for all students and approaches 20 percent for some ethnic groups.

As a society, we need to find effective ways to encourage more people to get an education and to assist them where needed. In the long run, this will have a positive impact on the have-nots.

In the meantime, the have-nots don't have to accept their circumstances or let the absence of an education hold them back. Uneducated immigrants come into this country every day. Many of them steer onto a road that leads to riches, and they become members of the Millionaire's Club. Opportunities are there.

From a macro point of view, better education should contribute to an even more affluent society. From a micro point of view, it should contribute to creating more wealth for more individuals. It should contribute to narrowing the gap between the haves and the have-nots and raise the overall level of income for individuals. It should contribute to keeping America in a world leadership position and minimize the risk our economy will lose momentum.

Policymakers and lawmakers need to continue to protect, preserve, and enhance our political and economic systems and address the gap between the rich and the poor. It's a pernicious and serious problem.

We need a growing economy to create wealth, which is what hard-working, enterprising people, who are pursuing their own self-interests, do. We're entering a political era where substantial social reforms will be discussed. We can't forget what has made America successful and wealthy. We should continue to try to make our system work better, but we don't want to change the fundamentals. Communism is a failure and it didn't create widespread prosperity. Individual initiative is thwarted or has no traction in such an environment. Modern socialism dampens individual initiative as well. But where democracy and capitalism coexist, the conditions, as history has confirmed, are right for individual initiative to be rewarded with personal success. Such success creates wealth for the individual and wealth for the nation.

Personal character is another element that plays a role in success. In the nineteenth century in New York, Horatio Alger, a Harvard-educated Unitarian minister and journalist, wrote a series of ten-cent novels intended to inspire the poor to succeed in life. His basic themes were always the same. Whether you were poor, orphaned, powerless, or homeless, if you would persevere, try your best, and do the right thing, you'd succeed in life. Honesty, hard work, and strong determination were the secrets to a better life. The American Dream was available to anyone who followed this formula.

Alger's concerns about the devastating poverty that plagued the ghettos of New York inspired his rags-to-riches stories. He became the nineteenth century's leading preacher of the gospel of success. Today, when a person comes from a disadvantaged background and becomes successful, we often say his or her story is a real Horatio Alger story. Oprah Winfrey's life is such a story.

Ben Franklin's autobiography and Alger's novels were examples of success through good character. For the past two hundred years, many commentators have emphasized that personal character is the key to success. These people advocate that persistence and hard work always lead to success. In the considered opinion of many commentators, personal character continues to be among the elements responsible for personal success. For many, hard work and persistence contribute to a successful life and, in some cases, are responsible for it.

Can hard work make you a success in life? Millions of people would answer yes. Will hard work alone make you a success? Reactions are mixed. Working hard at the wrong thing won't make you successful. You have to do something that produces wealth, and then hard work may make all the difference. The inventor Thomas Edison said success was 1 percent inspiration and 99 percent perspiration. Edison also said that most people miss opportunity because it is dressed in overalls and looks like work. Tom was one hard-working guy. I have friends and acquaintances who, like Edison, believe success isn't possible without hard work. Lucky people would disagree. Good fortune just fell into their laps.

For centuries, personal character has been regarded as an indispensable element in creating personal success. Some argue that persistence is the most powerful force in the world. Hard work, persistence, courage, dependability, discipline, enthusiasm, honesty, humility, honor, integrity, self-esteem, moderation, patience, politeness, prudence, respect, sacrifice, self-control, sincerity, tact, temperance, trust, and any number of personal virtues can be contributors to personal success. In a given situation, one virtue alone, such as persistence, may be the sole factor responsible for a person's success. In another situation, all the virtue in the world would be to no avail.

The Greek philosopher Socrates famously said, "Know thyself." Understanding who you are and knowing your strengths and weaknesses and talents and abilities is a good starting point to improve yourself and enhance your performance. I've seen all the aforementioned virtues exhibited, to one degree or another, in the successful people I've known. I don't recall anyone who possessed all of the qualities we collectively call virtue, but there are some virtues that present themselves more than others. Hard work would head the list. If you don't work hard, you're at a disadvantage, unless you're lucky, an heir or heiress, or a superstar talent. Determination and perseverance are often characteristics displayed by successful people.

Discipline is important. Most of us are capable of succeeding in life. If we don't succeed, it may be our own fault because we didn't do what was necessary. Individual initiative can be thwarted by extraneous factors such as health, discrimination, and disabilities, but sometimes it's because we didn't do our part. Do you have what it takes to make the trip to prosperity? Can you successfully travel one of the twelve roads to riches? Most of us can. If you find you're coming up short, keep working at it. You'll get better.

Be realistic and reasonable. We teach our kids they can accomplish anything they want in life. No matter how disadvantaged they may be, they can become president of the United States. Look at President Obama, the first African-American president. If half of the parents raising children told them they could become president, it'd be misleading at a minimum. Most kids won't get anywhere near the White House, even if their stated goal was to become president. Anyone may accomplish it, but of, say, fifty million kids, fewer than one hundred will have a shot at it during their lifetime. Most kids who've been told they can become president have no statistical chance of it ever happening. It's not realistic. Yes, we should teach our kids they can soar to significant accomplishment; but when a child becomes an adult, he or she needs to evaluate his or her possibilities realistically.

Sometimes we don't have what it takes to do a certain kind of work. Many kids want to be astronauts, but most don't possess the *right stuff*. If we don't have what it takes, we probably won't succeed. When I was young, I thought I'd like to be a singer. I've always wanted to sing. The problem is I sound like a wounded animal when I do. Had I pursued a singing career, I'd have failed. I don't have what it takes. It would've been unreasonable for me to pursue such a career. I know there are stories of musicians who aren't particularly talented but succeeded anyway. They're rare exceptions.

In other cases, we don't work hard enough, or can't make ourselves work hard enough, to accomplish our goals. In such cases, it's not surprising we don't succeed. We hear a lot about being passionate. Passion is a force that drives people to pursue their dreams and their goals. Passionate people usually work hard. You should be passionate about becoming a millionaire. If you're not, find an endeavor that comes easy to you. Author John Grisham admits he writes fiction because he says he's too lazy to write nonfiction. He doesn't want to conduct the required research. Short of inheriting wealth or being lucky, you must possess or acquire the virtues success requires.

Seek input and feedback from people—a parent, spouse, or sibling—who are interested in you and have your best interests in mind. Many times a teacher is responsible for one gaining insight into his or her capabilities and limitations. It could be a friend, co-worker, or boss. It's difficult for us to assess who we are and what we can do.

Sometimes others can help us gain that insight. An athletic coach is a great example. On a football team, a coach may move a player from offense to defense. The player may have always wanted to play halfback, but the coach puts him at free safety, and he excels. If the player is adamant about being a halfback, he can continue to work at winning that position by improving his halfback skills.

Have a close friend, business associate, or confidant help you know yourself better. Surround yourself with people who encourage you to do your best, get better, and use your talent. Embrace the army slogan, "Be all you can be."

Yet another element that may contribute to success is behavior. Dale Carnegie, author of *How to Win Friends and Influence People*; Napoleon Hill, author of the success classic, *Think and Grow Rich;* and other twentieth-century authors recommended a success formula based on personal behavior or actions. Stephen Covey captured this idea in *The 7 Habits of Highly Effective People* and enumerated what his research indicated you should do to succeed. Habits or behaviors, such as being proactive and engaging in emphatic communication are examples of the elements that contribute to personal success. Judging from Covey's tremendous success with his book, many people subscribe to this approach. Goal setting and developing a plan to accomplish your goals is a part of this behavioral approach. If you don't know where you're going, any road will take you there; but if you have a goal, such as entering the Millionaire's Club, having a plan makes sense.

One of the concepts Hill describes in *Think and Grow Rich* is a mastermind group. Successful people surround themselves with people who'll help them achieve their goals. A more contemporary concept is getting the right people on the bus, so to speak. Jim Collins makes this point in his best seller *Good to Great*. In a business, and in life, the people around you can have a huge impact on your successes and failures. Surround yourself with likeminded people, ones who need or want you to succeed. They share or appreciate your goals and see the value in them as you do. These folks may not always agree with you, and they may have different skills and perspectives, but their observations, comments, analysis, and overall input can help you tremendously.

Covey introduces his readers to the concept of synergy in *The 7 Habits of Highly Effective People*. He tells his readers to synergize. The term synergy comes from the Greek word syn-ergos, meaning working together. Synergy exists in biology and in physics. Two plants share one root system. You have one root that supports two plants instead of one. Two wooden boards nailed together will support a weight greater than twice the weight that each board would hold individually. This cooperation creates something greater than would have existed otherwise because of synergy. Surround yourself with the right people and extraordinary things can happen. If you're surrounded by the wrong people, you're much less likely to succeed. Humankind discovered early on that cooperating with one another and working on common goals made sense. Organizations were born, and remarkable things were accomplished.

GLADWELL

Malcolm Galdwell's recent best seller, *Outliers, The Story of Success*, adds valuable insights into the business of personal success. He points out that some successful people have opportunities and advantages that others simply do not have. This is especially true for those among us who experience extraordinary success. He points to Bill Gates as an example of one who had extraordinary opportunity. He also points out that our legacy; culture, background, and upbringing contribute to, or detract from, our ability to succeed. *Outliers* is well worth reading. It not only provides an explanation for some successes, but the information, upon reflection, is useful for self-analysis and self-improvement. It's a great book for parents to read.

For a person to put himself or herself in a position where he or she can succeed, he or she needs to develop competence over valuable work. Although washing dishes is necessary work it does not pay well. Brain surgery, on the other hand, pays very well. In chapter four I talked about mastery over work. A master is an expert in what he or she does, a skilled practitioner. Competence and mastery start with education and training but from there it is time at your craft and the experience you gain that leads to competence and mastery. Most of us need to learn to do something of value and do it well to succeed in life.

On January 15, 2009, we saw this competence and mastery displayed in a dramatic way when Captain Chesley (Sully) Sullenberger landed his disabled U.S. Airways plane on the Hudson River minutes after taking off from La Guardia Airport, saving the lives of all 155 passengers and the crew. Airplanes such as the one Sully was flying are not supposed to land on rivers. If you try to do so, it is usually a catastrophe. But Sullenberger made it look easy. The man has skills! If you take the time to read about the captain and his crew you'll find they were all well prepared to deal with the situation. The entire crew of Flight 1549 exhibited their competence and mastery over their work.

Ironically, you don't have to be an airline pilot, brain surgeon, the first violin in the Cleveland Orchestra, or a superstar of any kind to become a millionaire. People who rely upon thrift alone may do humble work and still become millionaires. The right employer can still make you rich even if your job is one that almost anyone can do. But competence and mastery are often associated with wealth.

MURPHY

Sometimes success comes quickly and with little effort. Most often success is elusive. Even those who set well-defined goals and objectives and prepare themselves for the task of accomplishing them, find that it is easier to state one's goals than to accomplish them. There will be obstacles to your success. You need to be a resourceful and a capable problem solver because Murphy's law predicts reality. If anything can go wrong, it will. A corollary to Murphy's Law is, inside every problem there is a bigger problem trying to get out. If things can get worse, they will.

The bad news is that you will have to solve problems on the road to personal prosperity. Your ability to solve them will define your success. The good news is that problem solving is one of the things human beings do very well. We start solving problems from infancy and continue throughout the rest of our lives. Actually, we're pretty good at it.

Problem solving was the theme of the Apollo 13 disaster. Well-trained astronauts were on a well-thought-out and well-planned mission to the moon when an explosion disabled their spacecraft. Solving the myriad of life-threatening problems that developed was a triumph of human ingenuity and teamwork. It is an amazing story. Although far less dramatic, millions of problems, great and small, are solved every day.

A couple of years ago I heard a talk Michael Simon gave to a group of small-business owners. Michael is a well-known chef. He won the Iron Chef competition on television a few years back. He operates two successful restaurants in Cleveland. His talk was about opening his second restaurant. The first was a great success. The second one should have been easy. It wasn't! Michael almost lost his shirt.

As he reiterated the story, it became clear that everything that could have gone wrong did. What was equally clear was that he had to quickly analyze the situation, identify the problems, and fix them. He did. But it wasn't easy. It was also gut wrenching and stressful. However, had he not solved those problems he would have lost a great deal of money, tarnished his reputation, put the first restaurant at risk, and disappointed his backers and employees. Michael is a great chef, a great entrepreneur, and a great problem solver.

Life is full of surprises and the road isn't always straight and wide. There are hazards and detours, bad weather and delays.

You will have to deal with them effectively to succeed. If you are not a good problem solver, team up with people who are.

A great book on the business of problem solving that advocates teamwork is *The Checklist Manifesto* by Atul Gawande, a physician. He illustrates, among other things, the necessity and power of involving other people in the process of solving complicated and complex problems.

He also points to a 1970s essay written by two philosophers, Samuel Gorovitz and Alasdair MacIntyre, about human fallibility. The question the essayists asked is why do we (sometimes) fail at the things we set out to do in the world? They observed that some things are beyond our capabilities and control. Human beings simply cannot do some things.

However, human history clearly shows we can do extraordinary things. But even where we can exercise control over outcomes we may fail anyway. Here, that failure, according to Gorovitz and MacIntyre, can be attributed to ignorance and/or ineptitude.

As it relates to ignorance, we simply do not have the knowledge or only a partial knowledge of the things we need to know to solve the problem. The general remedy for ignorance is education, training, and experience.

Ineptitude, our failure to apply knowledge that exists that would address or solve a problem, is our failure to perform. We make a mistake. We commit a sin of omission or fail to apply our skill correctly. In addition to education, training, and experience the remedies for ineptitude are practice, practice, practice, and process, process, process. Practice gives us mastery over things and process minimizes our failings.

The hero of Gawande's book is the humble checklist and the processes associated with its use, one of which is to extend a problem out over various experts for feedback. In other words, democratize the process of solving the problem. If you are not succeeding in life, not achieving your goals, share the problem with interested parties, those interested in your success, those who have a stake in your accomplishments.

Yet another place to find some insight into becoming all you can be is Malcolm Gladwell's book *Blink*. He points out the role that training and experience play in developing our ability to make rapid or quick decisions.

One last point; mistakes slow you down and can potentially ruin your chances for success. If you can avoid big mistakes, your chances for success may be enhanced and the potential for failure is minimized. Among other things (read Gladwell's *Outliers*), education, training, and experience will help you anticipate potential mistakes and errors and avoid them.

Decide what you'd like to do with your life and which road you'll travel to personal prosperity. Determine how you will create financial security in your life, and how you will become financially independent. Prepare for the task of succeeding. Get an education. Become financially literate. Take advantage of the opportunities you have living in a democratic and capitalistic environment. Determine your strengths and weaknesses. Continue to grow and develop in virtue and good character. Develop and embrace the habits and behaviors associated with success. Look for the opportunities in your life and exploit them. Develop competence and mastery over the work you chose to do. Hone your problem-solving skills. Avoid big mistakes.

The Elements of Success:

- Endeavor – Travel one of the twelve roads that lead to success.
- Environment – Take advantage of the opportunities available in a democratic and capitalistic society.
- Education – Get a college degree (if possible) and/or training.
- Character – Develop personal character/virtue.
- Behavior – Acquire the good habits and behaviors attributable to success.
- Competence/Mastery – Develop competence/mastery over valuable work.
- Problem solving – Overcome the obstacles that obstruct your success.
- Mistakes – Avoid the big mistakes.

CHAPTER 11
HOW TO BECOME A MILLIONAIRE

Rise early, work hard, strike oil.
— J. Paul Getty

The millionaires of the past acquired their wealth by successfully traveling one or more of the twelve roads described in this book. The millionaires of the future will do the same. Some future millionaires will inherit their wealth, while others will be lucky enough to win a huge jackpot or, by chance, end up with a membership card for the Millionaire's Club. Others will make a fortune in professional sports, entertainment, or media. Yet others will become celebrities, land big jobs, become doctors, lawyers, or hold other lucrative professional positions. Some will become millionaires by working for employers with generous benefits, while others will sell their way to success. Still others will become successful entrepreneurs and business owners. Some will succeed by saving diligently, spending carefully and enjoying financial security in the end. Finally, those who successfully engage in personal investing will find the security and financial independence they seek. Even some of those unscrupulous folks who travel the *Back Roads* described in chapter two will become millionaires, although the proposition in this book is that making an honest buck is the ticket to real accomplishment and personal satisfaction.

Several of the elements of success noted in the previous chapter—endeavor, character, and behavior—are summed up in Getty's quote that appears at the beginning of this chapter. I don't know if Getty's comments were a product of instinct or thoughtfulness. Perhaps it was a quip that contained more wisdom than he realized. Nonetheless, he rightfully identified behavior as an element required for success with his instruction to rise early. He points out that success requires the character displayed by a strong work ethic. He knew the value of engaging in an entrepreneurial wealth-creating endeavor with his admonition to strike oil. Getty, an American who graduated from Oxford, had the benefit of an education. He was a capitalist operating in the free enterprise system. His business accomplishments alone are testimony enough to his competence and mastery. Getty, like all of us, faced obstacles and problems that had to be solved in order to succeed.

Getty was also an heir. His father, an oil tycoon in his own right, died with an estate worth $10 million. However, he left Getty only $500,000. Nonetheless, this was a good start and helped Getty become a billionaire. But billionaires don't necessarily need an inheritance to become one. Bill Gates, Warren Buffet, and the Google guys didn't build their wealth on an inheritance. Neither did billionaires J. K. Rowling and Oprah Winfrey. They started from scratch.

At some point during a successful journey to personal prosperity, wealth manifests itself. It can happen gradually over time or it can happen in a single event. Your net worth, like Getty's, increases and, ultimately, becomes a million dollars or more in value. The exception is the equivalent millionaire introduced in chapter one and mentioned throughout this book. His or her net worth is less than $1 million, but he or she has acquired the income a million dollars would produce from passive sources, such as social security, a pension, and rents. He or she is not a millionaire but has a millionaire's income.

Progress toward the Millionaire's Club is measured by your net worth or acquiring its equivalent income. It's the metric you use to measure progress and success. It can be used to set your short-term and long-term goals. Your net worth is your wealth. It consists of the value of your assets minus your liabilities or debts. *It is what's left over after all spending.* If there's nothing left over, there's no wealth. What's left over takes many forms. Often it's leftover cash. In other cases, stocks, bonds, real estate, precious metals, or business assets represent wealth. Wealthy people often acquire other valuable assets, such as collectibles, artwork, and antiquities. For some wealthy individuals, employee and executive benefit plans, such as retirement plans and stock options, are the assets that represent all or a part of their net worth. Likewise, the right to receive payments under a contract, a pension plan, or social insurance programs like social security, as well as a legal settlement, rents, and royalties, are all assets included in your net worth.

At some point, when you no longer work to produce the income you need to pay for your living expenses, some of your assets will have to be dedicated to producing the income you need to pay for your standard of living and to purchase the things you need and want. How do you put yourself in a situation where there's a million dollars or more of leftover cash and other assets that can be used to produce all the income you need without working?

MONEY TREE

Countless parents have admonished their children with the phrase, *money doesn't grow on trees.* But it does, at least figuratively. Heirs inherit a money tree that someone else planted and nurtured. In some cases, these fortunate folks inherit an orchard. They simply pick money off the tree for the things they need and want and more money grows back to replace it. The accumulated wealth in a family that is passed along from generation to generation is invested in various forms. It is lent out in the form of savings deposits, bond purchases, and similar arrangements and earns interest. Some of the wealth is invested in stocks that pay dividends. Some may be invested in real estate that is leased out for rent, and some may be invested in private businesses that make distributions of profit. From time to time, some of these assets are bought and sold for a profit. Finally, the assets themselves, like a tree, grow in value; they appreciate. Certainly, the value of assets can depreciate from time to time as asset values have in the recent past. But history shows that the values of quality assets come back and grow further over time.

Some of the proceeds of accumulated wealth are used to provide the passive income heirs need to live and some is reinvested to make more money. The money tree yields its fruit and drops seeds so more trees can grow. And so it goes, money makes more money and the rich get richer.

The story for some lucky people and some beneficiaries is the same. They win, or otherwise acquire, a money tree. Then they and their children and grandchildren become heirs and live on Easy Street.

MONEY MACHINE

You are a money machine. Because you can travel routes 3 through 12 and endeavor in activities that allow you to acquire money, you are a money making machine. You can get paid for your efforts. The money you acquire through your active efforts pays for your standard of living and the things you need and want. Some money machines are big and powerful and can produce wealth very quickly and in large quantities. In these cases, wages alone are what make you wealthy. These high-income earners make so much money it is hard to spend it all. Granted, some do. But there are usually plenty of unspent wages and other earnings to plant an orchard full of money trees. For many professional athletes, superstar entertainers, some celebrities, and media personalities, as well as some executive positions, this is the case. Likewise, for most professionals, top salespeople, successful entrepreneurs, business owners, and successful investors, this is the case as well.

Those who regularly earn a solid six-figure income and many of those who have average earnings can save and invest enough to grow a money tree that will someday support them. The tree grows and multiplies over time and in the end produces enough for them to stop working and live off their accumulated wealth. Thrifty people will do this too. A money tree is your accumulated wealth. Once your accumulated wealth is sufficient to produce enough income to support your standard of living and enable you to purchase the things you need and want without working, you're on *Easy Street*. Many successful salespeople, those employed by a great employer, many of the self-employed, and smaller-business owners, along with those investing smaller sums of money, will, over time, accumulate enough wealth to enjoy financial security and independence.

If you don't inherit or otherwise acquire a money tree you can make money and accumulate wealth through your own efforts and use some of the money you earn and acquire to plant a money tree. Money machines and money trees produce wealth in the following ways:

- Earnings – Earnings include wages, interest, and investment income. The volume and frequency of wages one earns and the amount and frequency of interest and investment income one generates determine how fast you accumulate wealth from earnings.
- Profits – Profits are the result of successful business and investment activities. The volume and frequency of profits that one generates determine how quickly one becomes a millionaire from profit making.
- Appreciation – Appreciation is represented by the increase in value of the assets one acquires. Appreciation on assets increases one's net worth and contributes to accumulating wealth.
- Reinvestment – Reinvestment or compounding consists of taking interest, investment income and profit, and purchasing additional assets. The amount and frequency of reinvestment (compounding) that occurs with savings and investments, as well as in a business, makes a significant contribution to creating wealth.

The more you earn, the more profit you make, the more you save and invest, the more your assets appreciate in value, and the more you reinvest, the faster you will become a millionaire. Some roads to riches provide you with a bigger opportunity than others. For some the trip to personal prosperity is very fast and for others it can take longer—years or decades. Whatever the time, by successfully navigating the road to prosperity that you have chosen to travel, you'll get to your desired destination.

You start the process of becoming wealthy by creating earnings and profit in activities that have the potential to produce wealth. Travel one or more of the twelve roads discussed in this book. Never spend more than you earn or otherwise acquire. The interest and other expenses associated with going into debt can diminish your net worth and possibly force you to give up your assets to pay your debts. Avoid debt. You have to carefully manage the spending, expense, and debt side of your life to ensure some of your earnings, profits, appreciation, and compound growth are left after all spending. Remember, if there's nothing left over, there's no wealth. The more your money machine produces, the wealthier you will become. The more money trees you plant the more passive income you can ultimately generate. The road you choose to travel and the success you have navigating the route will determine how soon you become a member of the Millionaire's Club.

A reality check from time to time is very important. Periodically stop and count the leftover assets you have accumulated. Calculate your net worth. Is there cash in your bank account, in CDs, or an investment account? What's the balance in your 401(k) retirement plan? Has your business grown and is it generating free cash flow and accumulating cash? What is the value of your business? How much retirement income have you accumulated in Social Security and pension plans? Ideally, these assets will be growing in value on a regular basis. Accumulating leftover assets and growing your net worth should happen as frequently as possible; monthly or quarterly increases would be great but annually is fine. Sometimes it will take longer. That's fine too. As long as you are regularly doing the things that build wealth.

Don't count the value of your primary residence or the cars in the garage or the equity in a country club membership. They don't count. The only things that count are financial and business assets like cash, stocks, bonds, and real estate and other financial instruments and arrangements along with the value of your business if you have one. Serious collectables count too. I would not count a baseball card collection but a Picasso and maybe a '57 Chevy convertible represent items of unquestionable value.

MAKE A RESOLUTION

Resolve to live the life you want to live. Follow your dreams. Be passionate about life but have fun too. Be a well-intentioned person and act kindly toward your fellow man. Pursue happiness and personal prosperity. Live a profitable life and resolve that no matter what you do in life, you're going to become a millionaire and enjoy financial security and peace of mind. Engage in activities that have the potential to make you financially independent and provide you with economic freedom. Operate your personal financial life like a successful businessperson runs his or her business. Make a profit, get paid well for your efforts, generate and accumulate cash, save and invest and acquire assets of enduring value, assets that appreciate in value over time. Reinvest earnings and profits. Make certain there's always money and other assets left over after all spending. Avoid debt but manage it carefully where it exists. This is how you become a millionaire.

EPILOGUE

The current economic reality is disturbing. It's taking a toll on many. People are fearful. It would've been nice to finish writing this book during a time of peace, prosperity, and optimism, but it's no longer business as usual in our economy, our financial system, and on the job front. The system we relied on, and perhaps took for granted, has been shaken and our future, financial security, peace of mind, and happiness seem to be in jeopardy. The entire world, it seems, is infected with financial woe. It's difficult to believe the situation will improve—let alone that one can become a millionaire when benefits-rich employers and well-paying jobs are scarce—when:

- sales have plummeted and sales positions are being eliminated;
- great investors' portfolios are reduced by half or more;

- business failures are on the rise and entrepreneurs can't get financing; and
- thrift is a necessity and not a choice.

Once or twice in a lifetime, financial catastrophe seems to have its day. So we need to do what our forbearers, the colonists and pioneers did, and what our grandparents or great-grandparents did during the Depression: We need to be tough and persevere and increase our resolve, determination, and effort. We need to work through the mess, fix the problems, and build a better America, one with fewer financial meltdowns.

The economy will get better in time, and there will be other economic expansions and booms. It's only a question of when. It could take time. But don't believe for a minute that progress and prosperity are on a permanent holiday. Personal fortunes are being made as I write these words and as they will when you read them. Don't put your trip to prosperity on hold. Keep going. Work hard and don't lose heart. It's all right to offer a prayer too. Our forbearers didn't hesitate to pray in dark and difficult times. The quiet prayers of the many were often summed up in the public prayers of our leaders.

In his fourth inaugural address, Franklin D. Roosevelt said, "The Almighty God has blessed our land in many ways. He has given our people stout hearts and strong arms with which to strike mighty blows for freedom and truth. He has given to our country a faith which has become the hope of all peoples in an anguished world."

It is fitting and a hallowed American tradition to turn to the Almighty, pray for his grace, and give thanks for his blessings. It's appropriate to trust in God and his providence. It's consistent with our values to ask for God's help. It's as American as red, white, and blue. Our parents and grandparents often gave this advice. Work as though everything depends on you and pray as though everything depends on God, and everything will be fine. It's still sound advice.

In particularly difficult cases, desperate and troubled souls turn to St. Jude, the saint of hopeless causes and desperate situations. If he comes through for you, give him a public thank you as I'm doing here.

Today, as I finish this book, it's Independence Day, July 4, 2010. This is the day we celebrate our nation's independence and our individual right to pursue happiness and a better life. Although the economic uncertainty that surrounds us today is disturbing, it's worth remembering that America is and remains the land of opportunity. God Bless America.

ABOUT THE AUTHOR:

Tom Gilbride is the president of Gilbride & Company, a privately owned family business. Tom creates educational courses and conducts continuing education seminars for licensed professionals. He has created more than fifty courses and conducts dozens of educational seminars each year on matters pertaining to business, finance, and law.

In his thirty-year financial planning career, Tom worked with a variety of clients including individual consumers, employee groups, small and family business owners, professionals, and executives in both public and private companies. He is a Chartered Financial Consultant. You can contact Tom at: info@ gilbrideCE.com.